Publications of the

CENTER FOR EDUCATION IN LATIN

INSTITUTE OF INTERNATIONAL STUDIES

Lambros Comitas
General Editor

We Wish to Be Looked Upon
A Study of the Aspirations of Youth in a Developing Society
VERA RUBIN AND MARISA ZAVALLONI

Guidelines to Problems of Education in Brazil
A Review and Selected Bibliography
MALVINA R. MCNEIL

Black Images
WILFRED G. CARTEY

The Middle Beat
A Correspondent's View of Mexico, Guatemala, and El Salvador
PAUL P. KENNEDY

Telling Tongues
Language Policy in Mexico, Colony to Nation
SHIRLEY B. HEATH

Politics and the Power Structure
A Rural Community in the Dominican Republic
MALCOLM T. WALKER

Status and Power in Rural Jamaica
A Study of Educational and Political Change
NANCY FONER

Colonialism and Underdevelopment
Processes of Political Economic Change in British Honduras
NORMAN ASHCRAFT

The Dominican Diaspora
From the Dominican Republic to New York City—Villagers in Transition
GLENN HENDRICKS

The Dominican Diaspora

From the Dominican Republic
to New York City—
Villagers in Transition

GLENN HENDRICKS

Teachers College Press
Teachers College, Columbia University
New York and London

Library of Congress Cataloging in Publication Data
Hendricks, Glenn, 1928–
    The Dominican diaspora: from the Dominican Republic
to New York City—villagers in transition.
    (Publications of the Center for Education in Latin America)
    Bibliography: p.
    1.   Dominicans (Dominican Republic) in New York
(City)   I.   Title.   II.   Series: Columbia University.
Center for Education in Latin America.   Publications.
F128.9.D6H46   917.47′1′06687293   74-4203
ISBN 0-8077-2426-2

Manufactured in the United States of America

Photographs by Father John Oleaga and the author

Editor's Note

Rural migrants to the urban sprawls of the industrial world have long fascinated novelists, historians, and social scientists. The vicissitudes of life faced by these uprooted yet hopeful populations, their impact on society and its institutions, and the social problems that they have engendered have been extensively, vividly, and even luridly described. Understandably, much of this vast literature has focused on the migrant in his new setting—the newcomer in a host or receiving society. Only in the past few decades has the systematic study of migration shifted somewhat to questions of the impact of out-migration on the countries or communities of origin. And only in very recent years has migration begun to be viewed in a total or holistic context, taking into consideration the sending society, the dynamics of transplantation, and the receiving society. Glenn Leonard Hendricks' study of the Dominican diaspora, encompassed in the following pages, is among the first to utilize this new and productive thrust. Effectively employing the concept of social field, he deals with the circulatory movement of Dominicans to and from New York City, illuminating the dynamics of this process and its effect at both ends of the continuum. Aside from the serious methodological questions and reconsiderations that this book should raise for anthropology and other field-oriented social sciences, the case of Dominican migration should be of vital interest to educators and others involved in the practical problems of receiving, resettling, and dealing with thousands of new migrants, the newest wave of settlers to New York City that started only after the death of Trujillo. These migrants are in the process of working out a new way of life which includes residence in the United States but does not cut off effective ties and allegiance to their home *pueblos* in the Dominican Republic.

This is the ninth in a series sponsored by the Center for Education in Latin America, a series which attempts to bring forth the specifics of formal education and to offer materials and analyses that place the educational process in meaningful context. Geographically, the series concentrates on those political units, those nations, territories, and colonies south of the Rio Grande, commonly referred to as Latin America and the Caribbean. These constituent societies form a complex sphere that, with considerable theoretical difficulty, can be ordered into three culturally distinctive segments, a tripartite scheme that illuminates the heterogeneity of the area. Within each subdivision, uniformities in historical development, similar patterns of economic exploitation, and indigenous populations of approximately equal size and complexity have led to structurally homologous forms of social organization and articulation. Social institutions in each of these subdivisions, including those related to education, have developed distinctively regional forms and carry specific social significance.

One subdivision includes the territories and countries of the Antilles and the Circum-Caribbean. Characteristically, these societies contain institutions that bear the imprint of a long colonial heritage and a social legacy from forced connection with the metropoles of Western Europe. The populations of many of these societies have been derived primarily from Africa, but they also include important pockets of people with origins in Europe, the Indian subcontinent, China, and the Middle East. *We Wish to Be Looked Upon, Black Images, Politics and the Power Structure, Status and Power in Rural Jamaica, Colonialism and Underdevelopment,* and now *The Dominican Diaspora* are books in this series that concentrate on these island and coastal polities. A second subdivision includes those countries, most often located in the highlands of South and Central America, that contain large, culturally viable populations of Amerindians and in which the process of social and cultural integration of native peoples has dramatically influenced the course and form of nationbuilding. *The Middle Beat* and *Telling Tongues* deal with nations in the subdivision, a region sometimes referred to as Indo-America. The third subdivision encompasses the societies of the southern, temperate zones of the Western Hemisphere, which demographically and culturally are dominated by the descendants of migrants from Europe. *Guidelines to Problems of Education in Brazil* focuses on this region.

May 1974   Lambros Comitas

Prologue

They say Americans never speak of anything less than millions
and I said I would go and gather up the leftovers.
When I arrived there at dawn
I said, "This is a beautiful thing, I will become a Yankee!"

My family believes I am playing around and I was taken by the
    devil in New York.

My cousin Juan Maria met me at the airport (but)
Instead of inviting for a drink he took me to a factory.
The little that I earn I send to my wife.
I earn 48 and send them 26.

My family believes that I am playing around . . . [etc.]

She wrote me right away that I had already begun to drink.
Of the bundle that I earn I send 26.
Everyone who comes from there, this is what they believe,
They think that dollar bills are to be gathered up in Broadway.

That is what they believe, compadre.

> Text from *Un Cibaeno en Nuevo York,* by Luis
> Kalaff, published by Peer International Corporation.
> This is a merengue, a popular Spanish Caribbean
> folk ballad and dance form (translation mine).

Preface

The full meaning of those remarks customarily placed at the beginning of a book is rarely understood until the reader experiences for himself the role of authorship. Then he comes to realize the extent to which the final product depends upon the support, encouragement, and sufferance of others. My Dominican friends both in the village and in New York, although they must remain nameless, have been paramount in the success of this work. A special debt of gratitude is owed to Lambros Comitas of Teachers College, Columbia University; it was he who suggested the idea for the study and then combined those rare qualities of sensing when to listen and aid, when to guide, when to prod, and even when to avoid my questions and saw me through to publication. I also thank Gerald A. Murray, who coined the phrase "Dominicans in diaspora," on which the book's present title is based. And without the financial support of the Horace Mann-Lincoln Institute of Teachers College, this research could not have been undertaken.

The collection of date for this study was begun in late 1968 and the final editing of the manuscript completed in 1973. Attempting to keep the data current, especially in regard to census and immigration information, has been a problem because basic changes in U.S. immigration law were implemented during this time; these changes have resulted in significant shifts in the flow of migrants. Also, detailed 1970 census information is still being published at the time of this writing. I have tried to give the most current figures available but it is quite possible the reader will have access to more recently released information than is presented here. However, the same conditions of in- and out-migration, coupled with illegal residence, that I have noted in the book continue to plague with uncertainty any statement of population size.

G.H.

Minneapolis, 1973

Contents

Introduction

The arrival and dispersal of immigrant populations has been a basic theme in American history. The constant interplay between newcomers and the established order has resulted in patterns of accommodation varying from symbiosis to assimilation. The literature covering American immigrant populations is voluminous, covering a wide range of theoretical perspectives and disciplinary points of view. Recently, considerable attention has been paid to the Puerto Rican migration. However, attempts to explicate the patterns of acculturation and assimilation of Puerto Ricans as simply another cycle of the history of incoming ethnic and national groups have proved inadequate. Technological developments paralleling the post-World War II period of migration had great impact on these social processes. For example, no previous mass migration was accomplished by airplane. More important is the legal status of Puerto Ricans as United States citizens, free of the restrictions of United States immigration law. Further, this migrant wave parallelled a rising consciousness of racial issues within American society and the generally dark-skinned Puerto Rican found himself caught on the horns of the American Dilemma.

Focus of the Study

The Puerto Rican influx has tended to obscure the arrival of non-Puerto Rican Spanish-speaking foreign nationals, primarily from South and Central America and the Caribbean. The dimensions and nature of these populations remain largely unknown, although there is reason to believe that perhaps as many as half the Spanish-speaking population of New York City may be "other than Puerto Ricans." *

---

* The term "Hispano" denotes persons who are bearers of a culture complex that originated in Spain and speak Spanish. As used in the United States this usually includes Puerto Ricans, Cubans, South and Central Americans, as well as persons from Spain. Since there is no term in Spanish or English to cover just those

1

One such group of non-Puerto Ricans comes from the Dominican Republic. While the Dominican Republic has historically had close political and economic ties to the United States, the migration of Dominicans * to New York has occurred only within the last decade. The objectives of this study are several: to examine one segment of the Dominican immigrant group from a social anthropological perspective; to record the nature of the immigration and describe selected aspects of those social structural arrangements which reflect the process of acculturation, thereby placing it in the broader perspective of other ethnic and national groups in the city; to do so within the conceptual framework of the "social field," looking at both ends of the migration continuum; to indicate the implications these findings have for at least one of the major institutions of any modern society, the educational system.**

THEORETICAL CONSIDERATIONS

Increased interest in so-called urban anthropology, more specifically, anthropological studies done in urban environments, stems from many sources, not the least of which is the seemingly belated recognition by anthropologists of the world's increased urbanization. What is it that anthropology can add in the study of an area seemingly al-

---

persons who originate in Hispanic countries other than Puerto Rico, to make this distinction it is necessary to use some awkward phrase beginning with the descriptive "other." Official records in New York now usually break the categories down into "Puerto Ricans" and "Other Spanish." Until a few years ago this latter group was lumped into the general "Other" category, meaning all persons who were neither Negro, Oriental, nor Puerto Rican, thus further concealing this growing non-Puerto Rican segment. There is no generally agreed upon generic term for Hispanos living in the United States. Although used in Mexico in a derogatory sense, the term *pocho* (literally, faded or bleached) to denote Americanized Mexicans approaches the term that will undoubtedly some day be coined for all North American Hispanos.

* The term "Dominican" refers to individuals who are citizens of or identify themselves as bearers of the culture of the Dominican Republic. In most cases it refers to anyone from the Republic, although in this book it sometimes refers specifically to individuals from the village where field work was carried out. Any necessary distinction can be inferred from the context. I never heard anyone identify himself as coming from one particular village and rarely did people even say what region they came from. Rather they tended to say, "I am a Dominican" or, more frequently when they spoke in English, "I am from Santo Domingo." There are several reasons for this. Often they realize that the outsider is not familiar with the geography of the Republic. More importantly, many individuals do not wish to be openly identified as *campesinos* (peasants).

In everyday speech in the Republic the capital city is seldom if ever referred to as Santo Domingo, but rather as *la capital.* Santo Domingo is frequently used as a synonym for the Dominican Republic. Consequently, a number of teachers and other individuals working with Dominicans in New York refer to them as "Santo Domingans."

** "Education" is used here in its narrowest institutional sense as being synonymous with "schools," although I fully recognize that there are a host of other institutionalized forms of socialization.

ready well developed by other disciplines such as urban sociology and urban planning? The usual answer is that it makes unique contributions because of its cross-cultural and holistic orientation, even though in truth much of the work done in the field is neither. The pluralistic nature of urban life, however, with its complex multicultural components makes the application of the anthropological bias towards holistic considerations of cultural phenomena difficult.

Concepts such as "rural-urban," "primitive-civilized," and "ecological zone" have been used to understand cities as a whole, but they often obscure the cultural pluralism of the urban situation. *If we are to understand the city as a functioning whole, we must begin by looking at the different units of that whole.* Only then will we be in a position to develop conceptual models of the city as a unit . . . [to be compared with other kinds of settlement units be they city or village] (Spradley 1972:21, emphasis mine).

Without these building blocks of ethnographic description, the city will remain an enigma. This study is conceived as one such component in the eventual culture-mapping of New York.

In undertaking this study of Dominicans in New York City, I assumed that, as with the Puerto Ricans, modern modes of transportation and communication had drastically altered the nature of immigration to the U.S., and the processes of adjustment to the new environment. I further assumed that for full understanding of migrant behavior it was essential to examine both the social and cultural contexts of the sending and receiving societies, as well as the process of immigrating, treating each not as a discrete entity, but as a constituent element of one social field.

As the research progressed it became apparent that an understanding of the process of migration, including the implementation of U.S. immigration law, must come before any attempt at explicating the immigrants' behavior. Migration itself is an essential element in the formation and retention of linkages between the village and New York. In recent years there has been increasing public recognition of the problem of illegal alien workers in the United States. Hearings held in 1971 by a Subcommittee on Illegal Aliens of the Judiciary Committee of the House of Representatives revealed the extent of the problem: there are at least 2,000,000 illegal aliens, of whom 80 percent are thought to be Mexican, residing in the United States (U.S. Hearings 1971). New York City has many such individuals; few of these are Mexican, however. They live a shadowy existence for fear of detection and deportation. As will be shown later in this book, this marginal status has wide implications for understanding the Dominican and other recent immigrant populations of the City.

Social Pluralism: Its Implications for Dominicans

An objective of this study was to look for possible implications in its findings for those seeking formal institutionalized means to acculturate * "outsiders" to the larger American society. This objective would ideally require the ability to quantify the process of acculturation and to specify the patterns of relationships involved in assimilation, but at best, we can only make highly subjective judgments, arrived at through gross and relative observations. The real problem is in deciding the ideal against which to measure these processes. There are two possible models by which to judge assimilation. If we assume that immigrants are to be assimilated into an English-speaking culture, then the Dominican rate is very slow. If we view the U.S. as a pluralistic society, then the distance between the migrant group and one group of Americans with whom they are frequently identified— the Puerto Ricans—is not very great. The literature on Puerto Ricans in New York, based upon data accumulated in the early 1950's, leaves one with the impression that one could just as well be reading about the Dominican population in 1970.

The theoretical issues involved in defining cultural pluralism will not be discussed here. Rather, the reality of social pluralism is accepted as a valid assumption about the nature of American society, particularly New York City. Galzier and Moynihan have demonstrated the intergenerational continuity of ethnically based segments with the city (1963).

Acceptance of the validity of a pluralistic view of society leads to practical problems central and peripheral to the study at hand. The issue is central in that we are only belatedly coming to recognize the implications of that acceptance. The practical effect of legal and administrative decisions allowing acceptance of languages other than English for literacy requirements is slowly being felt on both practical and philosophical levels. For example, as a result of the administrative decision to grant New York drivers' licenses to individuals whose language competency is Spanish rather than English, it has been necessary to construct special examinations and to provide bilingual staff

---

* "Acculturation" has the meaning laid out by Redfield, Linton, and Herskovitz: it comprehends those phenomena which result when groups of individuals having different cultures come into continuous first-hand contact, with subsequent changes in the original cultural patterns of either or both (1936). "Assimilation" is seen as the relational patterns which are the result of the acculturative process. In a sense the terms "acculturation" and "assimilation" have the same relation as do the terms "culture" and "society." "Enculturation" in contrast is conceived as the process by which an individual acquires the culture of his group, class, segment, or society. "Socialization" is the behavioral aspect and generally is used as a broad term covering all these processes.

members. A pilot project in the administration of New York State Regents Examinations in Spanish raised serious questions within the city school system. To many teachers and administrators—as well as other citizens—the American educational system is one of the chief instruments for the acculturation of immigrant groups (Cremin 1961: 66–75). However, the validity of this belief, at least some aspects of it among the very poor, has been brought into question (Greer 1969). That the school has been instrumental in the process of acculturation cannot be questioned, but whether it has been central or crucial is more debatable.

This study has not been designed to determine the role of the school in the Americanization process of the focal Dominican group. Rather, it attempts to examine this group for social and cultural insights as to how the schools, as well as other institutions, might be more effective in their efforts to deal with Dominicans. It provides an explanatory framework for understanding the patterns of interaction that take place between Dominican patrons and the schools. The data are equally useful in understanding the group's relationships with other formal social institutions in New York City.

This study is concerned specifically with individuals who have come from the village of Aldea (a pseudonym) in the Dominican Republic, and generalizations will be confined primarily to this group. However, it is part of the larger segment of Dominicans who are in turn part of the total Hispano population in New York. It is necessary at times to speak of the larger segment to illustrate contrasts and to demonstrate the nature of socal relations within the total grouping. This focus on a relatively small group is a result of the methodology as well as practical considerations. Because of its limits, the study is not to be considered in any way an ethnography of a culture or classified as a community study, although it has elements of both.

Background of the Study

My interest in Dominican migration to and settlement in New York developed during a three-month anthropological field work training period in Puerto Plata, Dominican Republic during the summer of 1967. Here I became aware of the vast number of individuals who had relatives in New York City as well as the number who told me about their own visits or work experiences in New York. After I returned to the United States, I frequently greeted people on the streets of New York whom I had met only months before in Puerto Plata.

My newfound awareness of the Dominican population was coupled with an awareness of other Latin Americans—Colombians,

Ecuadorians, Peruvians, Cubans, and so on. An examination of available demographic data showed an almost total nonrecognition of "other than Puerto Rican" Hispanos. Because much of this group's immigration occurred during the 1960's, data from the 1960 census from which most population statements continue to be drawn failed to reveal their presence.

Several months after I had begun an intensive investigation of Dominicans in New York in late 1968 I began to realize how much larger it was than any official information would lead one to believe. The size and identification of this group was made difficult by a number of factors: the proclivity of English-speaking Americans to stereotype all Spanish-speakers as Puerto Ricans; the propensity of Puerto Rican leaders and agencies to claim for political reasons the entire Hispano community as their own; a Dominican social and political history which has taught individuals to value non-participation in any official attempts to identify or recognize them; and finally the presence of large numbers of individuals who live in the United States under the shadow of some real or imagined threat regarding the legality of their presence, and who do not advertise their existence.

During this time, it was frequently pointed out to me that one section of Queens contained so many individuals from a region in the Cibao (the northern portion of the Dominican Republic) that it was commonly referred to by the native village name. Initial attempts at gaining access to this group proved unsuccessful.

I then went back to the Dominican Republic and spent one month in the capital city, Santo Domingo, where I carried out library research and interviewed American and Dominican officials on aspects of migration to the United States. After that I lived for three months in Aldea. My work was greatly facilitated by the interest of the charismatic, socially active priest serving this area. His public announcements urging cooperation with my project eased early contacts with an otherwise hostile and deeply suspicious population; scarcely a family is not in some way implicated in visa violations. The help of a young store owner, who was one of the most economically powerful men in the community and had lived for eight years in New York, was of great importance; he sometimes asked questions of his customers for my benefit that I would never have dared ask.

During my stay in Aldea I came to know a number of individuals who were residents of New York but who had returned to visit family and friends. These individuals were instrumental in introducing me into the New York group when we returned to the city. Often they vouched for me, assuring skeptics that I was not an agent of the Immigration and Naturalization Service, and was in fact a *persona de confianza,* a trustworthy person. In addition, the parents of several large familial groups residing in New York validated my activities when they arrived in New York to visit their children. I am also indebted to the Spanish priest of a New York parish where great numbers of the people from Aldea are parishioners. He enjoys the confidence of the Dominican members of the congregation and his vocal support of my work helped me secure the cooperation of otherwise reluctant informants.

While at first I may appear to be writing about two discrete geographical and social entities, from the point of view of the individuals involved in the study both are parts of one field of social action. So closely are the events of Aldea and New York City entangled that one of the difficulties I experienced in writing has been to discuss one place without reference to the other.

RESEARCH PROCEDURES

While the bulk of the nonstatistical material was drawn from my activities as a participant-observer, I also tried to quantify some of the data through the use of a questionnaire. With a few exceptions, I found that informants from Aldea were considerably inhibited by my open use of a printed form. Although it was written in Spanish and designed to be either administered by the investigator or self-administered by the respondents, the functional illiteracy of most of my face-to-face respondents made self-administration impossible. Even those with whom I had much rapport answered items which they perceived as threatening or whose content they did not understand with evasion or misinformation. Part of this problem was resolved by my filling out the form from memory after an interview, leaving out items where I had failed to gain a specific piece of information. Thus, usable answers varied considerably from item to item.

The sample of persons who participated in this study was not drawn from a statistically random sample of either the focal group or the whole Dominican colony in New York.* The prevalent deep-seated suspicion of any outsider mitigates against randomness of inquiry.

The theoretical perspective of this study was of networks of social relations ** that operate in a social field. The center point of these

---

* It is difficult to use the term "community" for those persons from the Dominican Republic residing in New York; I prefer to remain with the term "colony" as it connotes far less interaction among members.

** This study does not attempt any further delineation of the concept network but rather uses it very much as Barnes did when he wrote of Bremes: "The image I have is of a set of points some of which are joined by lines. The points of the image are people, or sometimes, groups, and the lines indicate which people interact with each other" (1954:43). The use of the term "network" in referring to a set of relationships within a social setting has a long developmental history. The inquiries were the members of nine Aldean households in New York who were intensely observed as they interacted with others under a wide variety of circumstances. By tracing out the ever-widening network of interacting relationships, I was led to know several hundred individuals to varying degrees. They in turn were able to act as informants about many more. While a given individual's net may be fairly extensive, it remains almost invariably bounded by linkages established long before his arrival in New York. In addition, my research led to extensive involvement with other segments of the New York Dominican colony. Interacting with these persons, who were primarily from the urban areas of Santiago and Santo Domingo, allowed me to gain greater insight into the position of the focal group within the total Dominican immigrant group.

I have made particular effort to avoid using case material which in my judgement is atypical or is but a singular example. Interspersed throughout the text is exemplifying material drawn directly or condensed from my field notes. In some cases I have included more information than is essential for the specific point under discussion because I desired to give context to the event or person and also provide material useful in other discussions.

---

concept of social network has now been used in so many different definitions that "to insist on one definition of a network and one only, may invite confusion and hostility, not only within the ranks of social anthropology but also from those in other sections of social sciences, some of whom can probably stake a stronger claim to use of the term" (Kapferer 1969:192).

Part I
The Dominican
Background

ROOTS: *The tropical plain of the Cibao.*

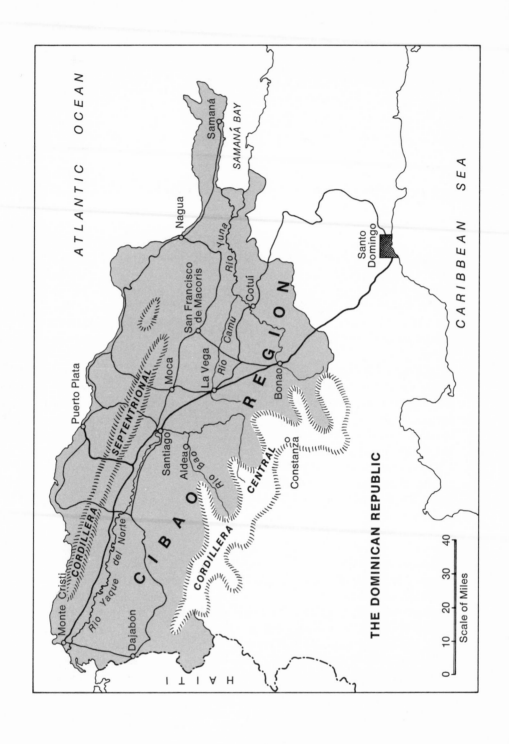

THE DOMINICAN REPUBLIC

CHAPTER ONE

National Perspectives

The Dominican Republic occupies the eastern two-thirds of the Caribbean island of Hispaniola, the second largest island of the Antilles. It shares a 193-mile border with Haiti, and is surrounded on its other sides by water: the Atlantic Ocean to the north, the Caribbean Sea to the south, and the 70-mile wide Mona Passage, separating Hispaniola from Puerto Rico, to the east. Santo Domingo, the nation's capital, is 1560 air miles from New York City and 849 air miles from Miami.

Geographically, the country can be divided into six distinct regions: the fertile, heavily populated Cibao plain in the north; the arid mountainous area of the southwest; the fertile but dry northwest; the eastern plain, characterized by its sugar plantation economy; the sparsely settled Haitian frontier; and the narrow southern littoral, dry but fertile in some areas, where irrigation is possible. Four rugged mountain ranges parallel each other from east to west across the Republic. They occupy most of the western part of the country, and have made transportation and communication difficult, contributing to the development of regional differences.

Over 40 percent of the nation's people live in the northern provinces, concentrated in the Cibao region. Historically the population of this area, especially around Santiago de los Cabelleros, the second largest city in the Republic, has been reputed to be wealthier, better educated, and more sophisticated than the rest of the nation. Most of the first wave of Dominican immigrants to the United States came from this region. It is in this region that the Catholic Church has its more active participants and therefore its greatest influence. The nineteenth and twentieth centuries have been marked by struggles between the north and south for political control of the Dominican Republic.

11

The Economy

The Dominican economy is basically agricultural. It is estimated that 60 percent of the population depends directly upon agriculture for support and that agriculture accounts for about 90 percent of the official foreign exchange earnings (U.S. Department of Labor 1968:3). Sugar products are the chief export items, but the sale of tobacco, chocolate, and coffee is also important. In recent years, with the growth of the large Latin American population within the United States, the export of such edibles as plantains, yucca, and meat to New York as well as to Puerto Rico has become important.

Bauxite from mines in the southwest is exported in quantity, and a Canadian mining firm has completed a sizeable plant in Bonao for the extraction of nickel from its ore, which is also mined in the region. Light industrial manufacturing for domestic needs is developing, but provides employment for only a small part of the work force. There are no statistics concerning unemployment and estimates vary widely. Ortega concludes that "between 14–15 percent of the total work force of the country [is unemployed]. This figure, however, does not include the extraordinarily high number of underemployed workers within the Dominican economy" (1971:6). The gross national product declined overall between 1962 and 1968. After Trujillo's overthrow in 1961, the GNP rose, but after the revolution of 1965 the economic situation suffered a severe setback. Since that time the national economy has recovered but the increasing population has further reduced the per capita income, which in 1968 was U.S. $275 (*The New York Times,* May 15, 1970). While the Republic's economy remains agricultural, this sector is hindered because approximately 45 percent of the total land surface is unsuitable for either crop-growing or cattle-raising purposes.

Demography

The population of the nation is largely rural. Sixty percent of the 4,011,589 inhabitants live in rural areas, that is, in settlements of fewer than 5,000 people (1970 Census). The average population density of 213 per square mile is high in relation to the circum-Caribbean area in general, but below the West Indian average. Haiti is twice as densely populated, while Puerto Rico's density is three and a half times as great as the Republic's.

Since 1920 the population has increased by 450 percent, a remarkable increase, although not as high as that projected during the preceding decade by the National Office of Statistics, which assumed an annual rate of increase of 3.6 percent based on the 1960 Census. "According to the now prevalent opinion, the basic explanation for the aforementioned decrease in the annual rate of population growth for the 1960–70 period lies in the substantial increase in emigration during the 1960's" (Ortega 1971:6).

As part of the expanding rural population has been forced to leave the land and seek employment in the Republic's few cities, the urban population has grown. These rural migrants go primarily to Santo Domingo, which now has almost 700,000 inhabitants, 17 percent of the nation's population. Santiago de los Caballeros, the provincial northern capital, has slightly more than 200,000 inhabitants.

TABLE 1. POPULATION CHARACTERISTICS OF DOMINICAN REPUBLIC

Year	Total Pop.	Urban	Rural	Urban vs. Rural %	%
1970	4,011,589	1,603,937	2,407,652	40.0	60.0
1960	3,047,070	922,090	2,124,980	30.3	69.7
1950	2,135,872	508,408	1,627,464	23.8	76.2
1940	1,479,417	266,565	1,212,852	18.0	82.0
1920	894,665	148,894	745,771	16.6	83.4

Source: Oficina Nacional de Estadística (ONE) 1967:5; 1970:29.

Historical Background

One must consider the Dominican Republic's history in order to understand present-day political events there and see how these relate to the mass migration of the past decade, as well as the love-hate feeling often displayed for the United States by the immigrants.

Hispaniola was the site of the first Spanish colonies in the new World; Santo Domingo was founded in 1493. During the first half century of settlement the island enjoyed great prosperity, primarily because of easily exploitable alluvial gold deposits and its geographic position as the focal point of Spanish New World activities. However activities shifted to the American continent, and the island's economic and political position declined by the mid-1500's. For the next 250 years it was left to stagnate economically and socially.

Attempts by the first settlers to enslave the native Taino Indians were unsuccessful; within two generations this indigenous population was almost extinct. The importation of black slaves was begun almost from the first years of settlement. During the seventeenth century French pirates and colonists settled almost unopposed in the northern and western portions of Hispaniola; in 1697 Spain ceded the western third of the island to France. As a result of the economical and political emasculation of this period the population of the Spanish part of the island dwindled to an estimated 6,000 in 1737, while at the same time the French colonists of Saint-Domingue imported thousands of African Negroes for work on their plantations. A major change in Spanish colonial policies in the mid-18th century led to a revitalization of the Spanish part of Hispaniola so that by 1790 there were 125,000 persons in the colony of Santo Domingo. Of these, 40,000 were white landowners, 25,000 were freedmen, and 60,000 were slaves. By then the French colony counted almost 500,000 Negro slaves in its work force (Roberts 1966; Franco 1969).

In 1801 Santo Domingo was captured by the forces of the momentarily liberated Haitian government and for the next eight years it was ruled by these French-speaking people of color. During this time the Spanish population decreased by one-third. Much of this loss was in the landowning educated classes. In 1809 the colony was once more restored to Spanish rule, only to be reoccupied by Haitian forces in 1822. For the next 25 years the country was economically and socially paralyzed as the black Haitians attempted to colonize the Spanish territory. In 1844 the Spanish population revolted and declared its independence from Haiti. The rest of the century was characterized by political upheavals, plots and counterplots, coups and countercoups. Leaders turned to Spain, France, England, and the United States, offering the right of annexation in return for protection and political support. Spain accepted the offer but was thrown out by another revolution in 1865, after governing for four years. The United States Senate in 1869 failed by a narrow vote to ratify a Dominican-proposed treaty of annexation to the United States.

Political turmoil and consequent economic chaos marked the succeeding years and in 1904 the United States sent customs delegates to collect duties so that defaulted international loans could be repaid. In 1916 under the pretext of helping to stabilize the political situation, U.S. Marines landed, and occupied the country until 1924. During this time

. . . the Dominican Congress was suspended, the Supreme Court stripped of its authority and the U.S. military governor granted power to rule by decree. The occupation forces improved the sanitation, communications, and educational facilities and engaged in other constructive projects, but the U.S. Marines assumed arbitrary power and at times abused their authority. Patriotic Dominicans of all shades of opinion disapproved of the occupation, and some engaged in a guerilla campaign against the U.S. Forces. . . .

Perhaps the more immediate effect was the creation of a modern unified constabulary, for it was through the constabulary that the future dictator,

Trujillo, was to rise to power. . . . It is primarily for this reason that the United States is still held accountable by Dominicans for the corruption and terrorism of the entire Trujillo era (Wiarda 1969:31).

The 31 years of the Trujillo dictatorship (1930–1961) left an indelible mark upon Dominican society. By maintaining tight personal control over the military and police forces, prostituting the political process, and establishing a near monopoly over the national economy, Trujillo was able to maintain stability and peace. But one consequence of this system was a disruption of the patterns of social stratification, caused by placing new categories of persons into traditional oligarchic economic and political circles. In addition, Trujillo was able to unify the political structure and thus concentrate political control at the national level. This has had wide implications in a society that has traditionally operated on the basis of patronage relationships.

After Trujillo was assassinated in 1961, the country once more lapsed into political instability. This led to the second landing of U.S. Forces in 1965. This U.S. interference and "occupation" during what is popularly referred to as the "Revolution," and U.S. support of conservative elements rather than the popularly elected liberal Juan Bosch, is still a source of displeasure to many Dominicans. Thus the nationalist, liberal, or leftist political aspirant who espouses anti-American sentiments can elicit considerable support either in the Dominican Republic or among Dominicans in New York.

Formal Political Processes

Political processes in the Dominican Republic reflect social forms characterized by reliance upon personal relationships and the dominance of individuals in leadership positions. Political parties reflect this *personalismo*, the dependence upon the personal qualities of an individual to attract followers. During the nineteenth and early twentieth centuries, historical and social events mitigated against the development of institutionalized political parties to serve as intermediaries between the government and the governed. The dependence on individuals rather than the more impersonal party was illustrated in the 1970 election when the Dominican Revolutionary Party (PRD), founded by former President Bosch, could not find a candidate to run against Balaguer after Bosch refused to run himself. Similarly, the precipitous death of Garcia Godoy two months before the same election left the National Conciliation Movement (MCN) unable to post a substitute candidate.

A visit to the National Palace provides a glimpse at the style of Dominican politics. Everyone knows everyone else personally or as a relative. Waiters pass in and out of the inner sanctums with little cups of coffee (*cafecitos*) on silver trays, as if government were little more than a constant series of family reunions. Indeed, favoritism to one's relatives and friends and self-aggrandizement from public projects are almost accepted norms. . . .

For those fortunate enough to have good connections, government thus becomes the vehicle through which privileges and favoritism are distributed; close friends and relatives entrenched in administrative positions customarily serve as the instrument of illegal advantage (Wiarda 1969: 169).

These cultural and social norms become important in the immigration process since it is difficult for a Dominican to believe that such a system does not exist within the U.S. Immigration Service and Consular staffs. Thus, *tributarios*, individuals who carry out the extralegal activities of helping an individual acquire a visa either in the Dominican Republic or in New York, are able to assure potential customers that they have the prerequisite contacts to obtain a visa.

Race

The great majority of Dominicans are mulatto, that is, of mixed white and black background.

TABLE 2. COLOR CHARACTERISTICS

Blanco (White)	12.1%
Negro (Black)	10.9%
Mulato (Mulatto)	77.0%
Amarillo (Oriental)	———— (less than 1.0%)

Source: ONE 1966:32.

The only numerically significant foreign population is comprised of about 30,000 Haitian Negroes (1960 Census), most of whom have come to work in the revitalized sugar industry. There has also been a significant influx of Negro British West Indians during the past century who have also come to work in the sugar industry.

Generally speaking, persons of dark skin color are concentrated in the sugar producing regions in the east and southern part of the country. In the Cibao region, especially the rural areas, whites or light-skinned mulattos make up the bulk of the population. The majority of Aldeanos, the villagers on whom this study focuses, are classified as *blanco* on their identification cards.

Racial attitudes in the Dominican Republic are expressed by a preference for "white" skin and the physiognomic features associated with it: straight hair, thin lips, and narrow nose bridges. However, socially derived attributes concerning family, education, and economic status are in reality more decisive characteristics by which racial categorizations are made. There is some discrimination against Haitians and British West Indian *cocolos* * but they are singled out more for their distinctive culture traits than for their generally dark skin color. The sharp racial categorization that becomes one of the early crucial issues of life for a Dominican in New York does not exist in the Dominican Republic.

Education: An Overview

The Dominican Republic claims the first university in the New World, founded by Papal decree in 1538, the predecessor of today's Autonomous University of Santo Domingo (UASD). The history of this university, as well as that of institutionalized formal education in general, mirrors the historical, political, and economic fortunes of Santo Domingo. In the sixteenth century, the university all but disappeared and during the period of Haitian rule in the nineteenth century, it closed completely. After the country became independent in 1844, education passed from church to state control, and the political disturbances of the modern period are reflected in the development of formal education.

Historically, formal education was a privilege reserved for the upper classes, who attended private Church-operated schools or were sent abroad, primarily to Spain and the United States. A system of publicly sponsored mass education, first planned by the Puerto Rican educator Eugenio M. Hostos in the late nineteenth century, has been handicapped by political, economic, and social considerations.

When Trujillo came to power in 1930 . . . there were very few public schools, and most of the people were illiterate. During his regime some progress was made in the construction of new schools. Emergency schools, principally one-room huts, were built in rural areas where formerly there had been none, and a few modern schools constructed in the capital. Nevertheless, at the end of the Trujillo era, there were 350 children of primary school age for each primary school, the average capacity of which was 40 pupils (Roberts 1966:113).

A national literacy campaign in 1943 was followed in 1953 by an adult literacy program which required adults to attend literacy classes;

* *Cocolos* refers to British West Indians who have retained major portions of the cultural patterns, including English patois, they brought with them when they settled in sugar producing regions of the Republic. One explanation of the term's derivation is that it is a corruption of Tortola, an island from which many of the West Indians originated. See Hendricks (1968) for attitudes concerning the *cocolos*.

the campaigns were only partially successful. The harsh measures taken to force attendance alienated many individuals. In 1967 it was estimated that about 50 percent of the population could be classified as illiterate. According to sample surveys taken in the same year, the urban areas of Santo Domingo and Santiago generally contain the highest proportion of literate individuals, and the economically depressed and isolated areas along the western border the lowest (*Dirección General de Educación Adultos* 1968). It is significant that the Central Cibao, from which the largest number of New York immigrants come, has a higher overall literacy rate than any other region of the Republic.*

THE NATIONAL EDUCATIONAL SYSTEM

The basic framework of the national educational system provides for *oficial* (public) schools entirely financed and administered by the national government, and *semioficial* (Catholic) schools which are given government financial assistance and meet government requirements. In addition, there are *particular* (private) schools, both secular and Protestant, which must follow prescribed curriculums although they receive no financial aid. School attendance is compulsory from the ages of seven to fifteen in areas where public schools exist; the lack of physical facilities and trained personnel make this requirement unenforceable. Because of the shortage of trained teachers, only 20 percent of classroom personnel meet minimum legal qualifications as licensed teachers (AID 1967:2).

In normal educational sequence an urban child would attend a six-year primary school, then go on to two years of intermediate school and four years of secondary school (*liceo*) to gain a diploma, the *bachillerato*. With this diploma he could enter the university. The whole educational system is aimed in both content and structure at preparing students for this level. A parallel system, with lower standards of teacher preparation and curriculum, exists in rural areas. Here the *cursos* (grades) offered rarely go beyond the third elementary level. In the past a child seeking more education had to transfer to an urban center. Even today only 5.5 percent of rural schools extend to grade six. In certain rural areas—Aldea is one—one school has been designated as a central school for a cluster of rural schools; children are sent to the central school for upper classes through grade six.

The rapidly expanding population has made it impossible to main-

---

* The looseness with which literacy is defined was indicated by one school teacher in Aldea who had served as a census taker for that region. She indicated that literacy was determined by asking the informant if he could read and write his own name. Another Aldeano present at the time of this conversation said that the census was seen as a threat by his father who feared he would be required to go to literacy classes if he said no.

tain the current level of accommodation, much less to expand it. In 1960 it was estimated that 73 percent of all elementary-age children were enrolled in school. By 1965 the percentage had dropped to 64 percent and projections indicated that in 1970 the total would be only 60 percent, even though the actual numbers of students and class-rooms would have risen considerably (AID 1967:1). Ninety-two percent of all Dominican children who enter the first grade drop out before they reach sixth grade. Examinations given at the end of each year provide major hurdles for most pupils and the rate of grade repetition is extremely high. In urban schools, 35 percent of the pupils repeated first grade during the school year 1967–68; in rural schools, 42 percent of those enrolled were repeaters.*

PUBLIC VS. PRIVATE SCHOOLS

The early development of privately supported schools, especially those operated by the Church, and the restriction of these schools to the more affluent classes, together with the historical deficiencies within the public system, have resulted in a general consensus among Dominicans that private school education is by definition superior to that in any public institution. The private schools are generally better equipped, teacher-pupil ratios are lower, and the level of training of teachers higher.

TABLE 3. CATEGORIES AND ENROLLMENT OF SCHOOLS IN THE DOMINICAN REPUBLIC

	Primary (pupils)	(schools)	Intermediate (pupils)	(schools)	Secondary (pupils)	(schools)
Urban:						
Oficial	185,966	220	17,923	129	26,853	63
Semioficial	28,145	123	5,579	80	7,927	72
Particular	24,785	166	4,107	59	3,731	37
Rural:						
Oficial	332,477	3,312	5,400	124		
Semioficial	21	1				
Particular	1,073	8				
Calendario *	76,106	940				

Source: Secretaría de Estado de Educación 1968:I-1.

Note: *Calendario Cafétalero* schools are those with a special school calendar from January to October, to avoid conflict with coffee harvest periods.

* Appendix C dramatically demonstrates the high dropout rate and the frequency of repetition of grades among those who do remain. By breaking the enrollment figures down according to school classification, it is possible to see the significant differences between these categories.

Teaching at all levels relies heavily upon memorization and repetition. There is little effort to elicit pupil initiative and independent thinking. Recent attempts to reorganize the educational program, especially at the secondary and university level, in order to produce more trained individuals to meet national social and economic needs, have been only partially successful. The traditional pattern places primary emphasis and value on the honored professions of law, engineering, and medicine on the university level and white-collar work in bureaucratic positions at lower levels. Programs aimed at increasing the number of trained technicians, for example, meet with great resistance. The national government has been hard pressed to raise sufficient resources to maintain the existing system, much less to expand or change it.

POLITICIZATION OF STUDENTS

The politicization of secondary and university students has further impeded those who see educational institutions as instruments of orderly social and political change. Much of the impetus for revision of traditional organizations and practices has come from outside "experts," chiefly from the United States. This has led to school strikes and charges of "Yankee cultural penetration" (see *El Caribe,* February 20, 1969, for a description of one such strike action). During the six months prior to the election of May 1970, the entire national school system was twice shut down for one-month periods because the government wished to avoid confrontations growing from student dissatisfaction with the party in power. The newly built Universidad Católica Madre y Maestra in Santiago has attempted somewhat vainly to avoid the threat of student activism by limiting students' involvement in university and civil processes. One of the reasons frequently given by students and would-be students for preferring UASD to Madre y Maestra is not only the prestige of the former, but, more importantly, the sense of political impotence that attendance at Madre y Maestra implies. Unfortunately, the open participation of U.S. citizens in the administration of this institution leaves it open to student charges of CIA activity and "Yankee imperialism."

CHAPTER TWO

The Village of Aldea

The previous chapter considered aspects of Dominican history and culture of which most villagers in Aldea are only dimly aware, despite the importance of these events and societal forms to their lives. We turn now to an overview of the village area and a physical and social description of it.

The Setting

Aldea is located some 28 kilometers southwest of Santiago de los Caballeros on an upland piedmont just north of the rugged Cordillera Central. A macadamized road has connected the village to the city since 1951, although a roadway of sorts existed for many years before that. The relatively flat plateau on whose edge the village is located ends precipitously at the Bao River, a substantial stream on which a dam was built in 1969. The Bao joins the River Yaque six kilometers downstream.

Most of the village itself is on a bluff 200 feet above the river and houses adjacent to this bluff have a panoramic view up the river valley to the increasingly rugged mountain ranges beyond. The land immediately surrounding the village is intensively cultivated; yucca, plantain, sweet potatoes, and a poor grade of tobacco are the main crops. About a quarter of the land is given over to cattle grazing. The landscape is irregular, cut with deep ravines, and the soil is uneven in its fertility; crops grown on one small plot may not be suitable for the adjoining few *tareas* (one *tarea* = .154 acres).

Scattered in the nearby hills are other small settlements, most connected to the main road by unpaved, ungraded roadways carved into the steep hillsides. These are passable only to four-wheel drive vehicles during the dry season. Another settlement lies across the river but there is no bridge; it is possible to ford the dam by walking or driving on its apron when the water is not too high. From this point on transportation is almost exclusively by animal or foot. Aldea is literally the end of the road into the region.

Since this region was settled a century ago, Aldea has been a trading center and collecting point for such agricultural and forest products as the *campesinos* had to trade, especially tobacco and woven palm products. Prior to the 1870's the area was devoted exclusively to cattle ranges as part of a large *hato* or cattle ranch.*

At about this time three members of a family of white Spanish settlers gained possession of the land and began more intensive cultivation. The lineages formed through a variety of unions of the original settlers were extensive. The number of individuals acknowledged as descendants of the three families differs from informant to informant, depending upon which unions they recognize. Even today a single individual male may acknowledge paternity of dozens of children. Dominican legal and social codes which assume equal inheritance rights, coupled with the large numbers of offspring, have resulted in the division of land into ever smaller plots, many too small to support a household. Intermarriage of first cousins is valued and frequent, especially among landholders, as it functions to prevent the further division of landholdings.

The oldest buildings in the village, two large wooden houses located at the end of the paved road adjacent to the village's tiny park, date from about 1910. The old school, built in the 1920's, and the first church building were nearby, but both structures were replaced by newer ones on more spacious plots at the other end of the village. The remaining area facing the park is built up with two shops, an *almacén* and a *bodega*,** and a newly built restaurant. Nine more businesses, including other foodshops, a barber and tailor shop, and a cobbler are found in the village.

The most significant single event in the village history came in 1960, when the dam was built across the river and a pumping station installed to draw off water for the Santiago municipal water system. The year-and-a-half construction period brought in large numbers of outside workers, some of whom stayed on to operate and maintain the dam. To guard it, a small national police garrison was established; this of course brought in more outsiders. The electrically driven pump

---

* See Antonini (1968) for a discussion of the changing ecology of this region as a result of its settlement over the past century.

** An *almacén* is a store primarily for foodstuffs, and serves both retail and wholesale functions. In contrast, the *bodega* is a retail store only. Ownership of the *almacén*, since it must stock larger quantities, requires the control of far greater quantities of capital. In the case of these two stores, the *almacén* also stocks some building materials, while the *bodega* stocks some articles of clothing and purchases cured tobacco in the form of *guandule*. The owner of the *bodega* was both father-in-law and uncle to the owner of the *almacén*.

motors necessitated the construction of power lines to the area. Consequently, Aldea and the immediate area have both a dependable hygienic public water supply and uninterrupted electricity, two things which make it atypical of most of the *campo* and even of many urban neighborhoods.

The village serves as the focal point for economic, religious, communication, and education activities in the area. The *almacén* serves as supplier to *bodegas* located in the countryside. Aldea * is also the postal address for an area of about 100 square kilometers, and individuals must come to the post office to pick up their letters. The school is a designated district school and in 1969–70 had classes through grade six. Four surrounding settlements have their own schools for the first three grades; older children walk to Aldea to attend the higher classes. The Catholic Church is another important centralizing institution as it is the focal point of all religious activity in this highly religious area. As the end of the paved road into the area, Aldea is a collecting point for the *carros públicos* (taxis) that travel to Santiago and Santo Domingo.

The traffic to Santiago is considerable. All governmental business —other than postal and educational—must be carried out in Santiago, since it is the seat of local as well as provincial government. With the exception of a once-a-week visit to Aldea by a dentist, medical and dental facilities are available only in Santiago. A favorable one percent differential in the black market value of foreign checks and cash exchange in Santiago rather than in Aldea makes the one peso cost of the round trip worthwhile for those who receive remittances from the United States.** In addition, Santiago shops afford a much wider variety of merchandise than is available locally. Even though Aldea is the end of the road, during daylight hours one need never wait for more than half an hour for a taxi to Santiago. At least one car travels daily to Santo Domingo and its airport, carrying passengers destined for and returning from New York. This daily contact with New York is noteworthy, for it exemplifies the intimate linkage that exists between the two widely separated places.

* It must be recognized that Aldea is legally defined as a postal unit, a political unit called a *paraje*, and a larger unit called a *sección*. It is socially defined as an area composed of either one or all of these, according to which person and place reference is intended. In New York the postal unit is the usual reference to an outsider, including other Dominicans; locally the *paraje* is the frame of reference. Thus, of the several thousand persons said to be from Aldea only some come from the village itself. This description confines itself to the geographical area of the locally defined *paraje*, or village, boundaries.

** Since 1947 the value of the Dominican peso has been kept at a par with the United States dollar (RD$ 1 = US$ 1).

Migration to New York

The migration of one of its sons to New York as early as 1939 had a far-reaching effect on Aldea. His migration was successful but apparently no one followed him until 1946, when he helped a much younger sister join him in New York. She in turn assisted in bringing up other relatives from the village, including two young males, her spouse's children from another union, by providing financial assistance and acting as sponsor. Undoubtedly others may have ventured north, but this woman, who retired on social security and now lives in the village, is pointed out as the first one from the village to have gone to New York. The first sizable migration seems to have taken place in the mid-1950's, expanding considerably after Trujillo's death, when emigration became easier. It is important to note that the phenomenon of this migration preceded that which developed in other parts of the Republic by almost a decade.

PHYSICAL EVIDENCE OF MIGRATION

The impact which the migration of Aldeans to New York has had upon the village is widely evident. Houses and business establishments are sturdily constructed of concrete blocks or wood, topped with bright metal roofs; these substantial structures indicate a higher level of economic development than villages in other parts of the Republic have reached. Some houses, locked and shuttered, await their New York owners' return. In almost every case present or past residents of New York have constructed these buildings. During my residence in the village, the one local builder completed a large house for an elderly couple (paid for by their children in New York), started construction of a restaurant building for a New York returnee, and had agreed to build two other concrete block houses to be paid for with New York money.

Another visible sign of the villagers' prosperity is the cemetery. Expensive and massive masonry family tombs have been constructed with money accumulated by Aldeanos who at some point in their life cycle have lived in New York. As one villager said, "Everyone expects to come back, one way or another."

SOCIAL AND ECONOMIC EFFECTS OF MIGRATION

The migration phenomenon has had more than a physical impact upon the village. Sociologically and economically, it has transformed it and the area around it from a self-contained and rustic rural community to one whose culture and social organization are more directly tied to New York than to Santo Domingo. The social network and economic resources of most Aldeanos are intimately connected to both countries. In many senses the village is an economic and social appendage of New York and vice versa.

There are always individuals in Aldea who have lived, are living, or hope in the near future to be living *allá.** Within the boundaries of what is generally recognized as the village of Aldea are 146 households. Eighty-five percent of these have one or more immediate family members (mother, father, sons, or daughters) living in New York. Households without such relatives are those whose members are not native to the village, but have moved there because of the construction of the dam or because migration has made housing and some job opportunities available.

Doña Ana and her husband Bobo, both in their 60's, have just built a new three-bedroom masonry house with funds sent by five children living in New York. One son has been the chief contributor and it is recognized that he will have first claim to inherit the house. Doña Ana is the most respected person in the village. Even though she and her husband are unimportant in economic affairs as either property or store owners, she can trace effective kin relationships to most of the families with money (*los que tienen*) in the area, and in her position as moral leader of the community exercises a degree of moral suasion with them. She has been in New York three times visiting her children and during two of these trips collected funds for the new school among the immigrant Aldeanos. Bobo holds an invalid residence visa for the U.S. which he claims to have gotten only because his children insisted, so that he could use it to "ask" for visas for his children. He once lived in New York for a two-month period.

Nina, 25, lives with her four children in a rundown house next door to Doña Ana. Her legal husband works in New York as a dishwasher and contributes irregularly to her maintenance. He has for the past three years been returning home each winter for several months, leaving his children newly clothed and his wife pregnant. Except for beds in the bedroom, the house is almost completely barren of furniture. Nina in the past attempted to run a small *bodega* in front of her house but now all that remains is a giant refrigerator with a few bottles of beer and soda pop. She is not from the village, but from some 50 kilometers away. Her husband is a native, however, and his lack of responsibility in caring for his family is the subject of a great deal of gossip. Some of his family members aid her and infrequent nocturnal male guests contribute to her maintenance.

Rafael, 55, and his wife have lived in New York for eight years, both working in clothing factories. In 1967 they built a substantial wooden house on

---

* In ordinary conversation one seldom hears New York or the United States referred to as *Nueva York* or *Los Estados Unidos,* but rather as *allá* (up there). Also, as Gonzales points out, "it is noteworthy that the Dominican informants in their own country speak of the United States as though it were New York (1970: 162).

land which Rafael bought from his aunt. It is his intention to save enough money to return permanently. Presently they return each winter for from one to three months and live in the house. The rest of the time it remains locked and shuttered, watched over by relatives who live next door.

Lottie and Juan, first cousins and direct descendants of the original settling family group, are middle-range land owners. They have six children living in New York. Neither has any desire to live permanently *allá* but both visit their children often, and vice versa. They have accumulated some capital and Lottie is one of the minor money lenders in town, primarily for persons desiring to go to New York. Her lending arrangements are conducted on a less aggressive basis than most. Her rates of interest are generally less than other *prestamistas* and there is less gossip about her activities than most other known lenders.

DEMOGRAPHIC EFFECTS

Another effect of the migration to New York has been the skewed distribution of the age of the population that remains. In the village itself, and to a much lesser degree in the surrounding areas, the population consists of the young and the old. The mean age of heads of household interviewed was 51.5 years. This is in sharp contrast to the fact that less than ten percent of the national population is 50 years of age or older (Latorre 1969:51). Fifty percent of the total sample I investigated was fourteen years old or less. A census made earlier in the same year by school officials revealed the same distribution; national population statistics indicate that about 47 percent of the national population is in this fourteen and under category. The missing group in Aldea is that between eighteen and 45, the age when migration to New York to obtain work is most feasible. For the most part, eighteen-to-45-year-olds in Aldea were: those who had moved into the village from the outside, whose occupations usually involved employment with such outside agencies as the post office, the waterworks, taxi drivers, and the police constabulary; those who had lived in New York and returned either permanently or temporarily to the village; those who through physical or social disability could not get U.S. visas; females who remained with their children. In one case a male was paid by five of his siblings who lived in New York to remain in Aldea to watch over family land interests and be responsible for the many children left behind. While these children did not live with him, he received monthly remittances from their parents and paid the households in which the children lived.

This denuding of the adult population has had serious repercussions in the recruitment of individuals to fulfill necessary social roles. Leadership in communal activities normally carried out by this age cohort must be filled by older persons and newcomers. Thus, the two most respected individuals in the community were the 68-year-old doña Ana, and don Raphael, an employee of the waterworks, who had lived in Aldea for only five years.

EFFECTS OF MIGRATION ON LEADERSHIP AND POLITICAL ACTIVITY

Attempts by concerned agencies to develop new local leadership results in developing aspirations to go to New York that might otherwise have remained latent. Several years ago *Oficina Desarrollo de la Comunidad* (ODC) leadership training was given to a young man from a nearby settlement who was judged to have potential leadership qualities, and he was sent to Constanza for a training course. Shortly after he returned, he applied for a vistor's visa to the United States and went to New York where he worked illegally. There he saved enough capital to return to Aldea and buy a vehicle that serves as a taxi and delivery wagon in the rough terrain off the paved highway.

There are no medical facilities in Aldea and no one sufficiently trained to give even the most rudimentary nursing care and medical information. The local schoolmaster and one other person own hypodermic needles and give injections, but the extent of their training and understanding of what they are doing is extremely limited. Padre Ricardo, the local priest, organized a *cursillo* (short course) for practical nursing training in the village, taught by nursing personnel recruited from the university in Santiago. For a month before the cursillo began he announced at each Sunday mass that he was recruiting fifteen persons to take part in this intensive two-week course. The one stipulation was that participants could not be planning to go to New York. Eventually thirteen women took the training and received certificates. Six months later five of them were in New York.

The people of Aldea do not generally take part in formal political activities, although some of the wealthier landowners contributed to the Partido Reformista (PR). One resident who had risen to the rank of colonel under Trujillo was said to be a would-be *tributario*, but his inability to expedite the visa procedure had largely discredited him in the eyes of all but the most unsophisticated *terrenos* (small plot agriculturalists). In contrast to urban areas, where discussion of political affairs is frequent, open, and sometimes violent, the conversation of Aldeanos seldom touches on such affairs. There is no formal political organization representative, no posters, not even any of the crudely scrawled political slogans on the walls of buildings that one commonly sees in the cities and provincial towns, or even hamlets in other parts of the Republic. Pictures of President Balaguer and Vice-

President Lora of the Partido Reformista became visible only after PR representatives from Santiago arrived with a truck and car carrying party functionaries, a liberal supply of picture calendars, and a limited quantity of rum. These were distributed to a small crowd of men and children hanging about the town park and post office. The politicians greeted no one specifically, and no resident showed any interest beyond getting what was being handed out.

On the few occasions that political matters were discussed in my presence, it was generally to speculate about what would happen if Balaguer were not reelected—it was feared that social, economic, and legal disruptions like those of the Revolutionary period would return. In keeping with its overall conservative nature, the *paraje* (district) of Aldea voted overwhelmingly in favor of Balaguer in the 1966 election. The people of Aldea assumed his election would mean the return of the peace and tranquillity they remembered from the Trujillo area. One of the frequently cited reasons for the early migration to the United States from the area was that the apolitical behavior of the villagers resulted in few political reprisals, and hence fairly easy access to passports: "He had no reason to keep us here; we had no money, we had no power." It is the consensus of most Dominicans that obtaining a passport during this time was possible only through the payment of sums of money and possession of a "safe" political record.

The Catholic Church

Catholicism is the official religion of the Dominican Republic, recognized by a concordat with the Vatican. No public and few private functions are held without attendant Catholic religious functionaries. In general, in the Republic the regular participation of the population in church activities, attendance at Sunday mass, for example, is extremely limited. Some estimate that while 95 percent of all Dominicans call themselves Catholic, only ten percent actually participate (Wipfler 1964:2). However, the conservative villages of the rural Cibao cling tenaciously to the forms of Catholicism. While in other areas Protestant sects, especially Pentecostal groups, have been able to make conversions, the *campesinos* of the rural Cibao are not generally a fertile field for their proselytizing. In Aldea weekly Sunday mass is crowded to overflowing, with well over 500 persons in attendance. In addition, a midweek mass is well attended. *Cursillos,* or prayer sessions, are held by local lay readers two or three times weekly in the evening. At seven o'clock each evening, *novenas* are read over the national radio; scarcely a house in the whole village does not have the radio turned on at this time with families gathered about reciting in unison.

What formal organized communal activity exists in Aldea does so in the context of church activities and through sanctions of either secular or clerical church leaders. Historically, Aldea grew out of its position as a trading post as well as the site of religious services for the surrounding population. There is no resident priest, but one who lives in Santiago is assigned to an area of which Aldea is a part, and travels from congregation to congregation saying masses.

Overt leadership in the church and hence in the community is exercised by the appointed priest. The priest in charge at the time of my field work, Padre Ricardo, was an unusual, although not unique, representative of the young vital clergy emerging in the Dominican Republic. These priests are far more concerned with social activism than with the performance of traditional liturgical chores. While some have resorted to political activism, which places them in open confrontation with the government and the military, Padre Ricardo turned to the promotion of social welfare projects among his parishioners. He was born in the *campo* about 15 kilometers from Aldea, one of a large *campesino* family. An older brother studied for the priesthood and has achieved considerable distinction in the academic world of the Dominican Republic. Through this brother's influence, Padre Ricardo was educated in a church-operated boarding school and subsequently studied for the priesthood. Using both his brother's connections and contacts he himself made while studying in the United States, Padre Ricardo organized a private foundation called *Acción Social* to undertake social action projects among his rural parishioners. Money from U.S. sources has been used to purchase four vehicles, several portable generators, and motion picture projection equipment. Thus, each Saturday evening in Aldea, the residents look for the arrival of the truck of the *Acción Social* for the weekly movie. Most of the money for these activities comes through direct solicitation by Padre Ricardo of New York residents.

Padre Ricardo's constant emphasis on projects for personal or communal betterment did not receive universal approval; his deviation from the traditional role that the congregation expected of a priest was just barely tolerated. Typically negative remarks centered around his departure from the perceived priestly tradition and the forthrightness of his actions: "He pushed too hard. . . . His hand went too quickly to your pocket. . . . I never liked it when he talked about things that didn't belong to the Church. . . . We already have one *promotora* (government worker) living in the village whose job it is to develop community action projects in the area."

Padre Ricardo said the people of Aldea "are very stubborn, and still asleep. They are so simple. There is no one to be a leader here because those kind of people leave for New York. The young ones think only about going up there and the old ones only wait for their checks. Don't be fooled by seeing all those people coming together as a congregation in your American sense. Each enters and remains alone as he prays and asks for help for only what he wants."

Cooperative Activities

Adjacent to the church is another large building originally built to house a cooperative association organized to aid the *campesinos* in coordinated programs of buying and selling their produce. However, the coop failed, amid accusations that its officials had been involved in illegal activities. The building reverted to the church which now uses it for community activities as well as for small religious functions. Generally speaking, however, secular activities are confined to the *cooperativa* and religious ones to the *iglesia*. As in other aspects of these relations no clear-cut boundary exists. The community school meetings are held in the *cooperativa* on Friday nights, after prayer meetings led by the local teacher, or on rare occasions, after Sunday mass in the *iglesia*. Normally, the Saturday night movie is held in the *cooperativa* but when the crowd becomes too big the showing is transferred to the *iglesia*.

The suspicion and jealousy among villagers which led to the failure of the *cooperativa* is frequently cited as the reason that formal group activities, aside from the church, unless led by outsiders, which include the clergy, have little chance for success in Aldea. Probably a more realistic reason for the poor odds is the limited opportunity for such activities to exist. Until very recently the community consisted of a few related kin groups who were able to organize within themselves whatever mutual aid was necessary. Cooperation and mutual aid groups in some form were said to have been in existence until a generation ago, when farm plots were larger, but usually they were organized among kinsmen and *compadres*. The district cemetery is still maintained through *convite*, cooperative work groups, organized in turn by the *alcalde* (sheriff) of the various *parajes*. It was said that the work group for Aldea was the hardest to organize, but this may well be because the majority of individuals who normally participate in these efforts had left the village.

The building of the new school, dedicated by President Balaguer in the fall of 1969, was a major communal action. Although it was instigated through national government action which initially provided 50 percent of the total cost and provided a community organizer, the efforts of the community to provide its share, both in the form of donated labor as well as cash, cannot be belittled. However, much of the cash was solicited in the United States or from visiting New York residents. The village's economic leaders participated only minimally; one, the parent of a school-aged child, felt his payment of the committee-imposed head tax of one *peso* a month was enough of a contribution. These persons were consistently absent at community meetings called to discuss the school. A repeated comment concerning their non-attendance was, "They are afraid they are going to be asked for money."

Social Relations

In the Dominican Republic the extended family is undoubtedly the most powerful and fundamental social unit. One of the cultural traits enumerated by Wagley (1968) as part of the Latin American tradition is the emphasis on strong family bonds. In a country frequently disrupted by internecine political upheavals the family has traditionally been the one group in which strong bonds of trust and affection could be maintained. The implications of this for migrant activity are many, both in terms of financial obligations and the reception afforded the newly arrived migrant in New York. These familial ties are further strengthened by the force of immigration law which until quite recently placed great premium on such bonds.

In considering those to be included in the categorical concept of "family" (*familia,* or *parientes,* the latter term referring expressly to the extended family or kindred), one must include fictive kinsmen adopted through *compadrazgo* relationships. Although it is clear to Aldeanos that *compadres,* if selected from outside their *parientes,* are really not of the same *sangre* (blood), they recognize that functionally they are equivalent. *Compadrazgo* relationships, common throughout Latin America, refer to the establishment of strong emotional, moral, and social bonds between individuals chosen to be witnessing or responsible participants at the crisis rites, particularly baptism or a marriage ceremony. Not only is the relationship established between the *ahijado* (child) and his *madrina* and *padrino* (godparents), but between the parents and the *compadres* and *comadres* (co-parents). While the relationship between the child and his godparents is one of great esteem and affection, the bonds established between the two sets of parents are especially strong. Urban dwellers in the Dominican Republic often consider this relationship somewhat old-fashioned and rural. However, the practice survives at every level of society. Among people in Aldea the *compadre* is usually chosen from among one's kinsmen, reflecting strong family ties and distrust of those outside, but outsiders are frequently chosen. The respect and changed relationship is demonstrated by the mutual shift from the informal third person *tu* to the formal *usted* form of address, even to a brother with who one has grown up and always been on a *tu* basis. Sexual relations between *compadres* are considered incestuous. These fictive relationships become extremely important in understanding bonds of interaction that take place both in the village and in New York.

At all levels of society strong emphasis is placed upon trust, mutual aid, and familial solidarity. Individual members are socialized with a deep sense of collective responsibility for the acts of others. Members of a family share in the honor as well as the shame of the consequences of acts by one of its members.

It must be remembered that the Aldea area was originally settled by several members of one Spanish family five generations ago, and in many ways the community can be viewed as one large kindred. However, this unity has broken down and a number of "stem kindreds" (Whitten 1965) have emerged. The wealthiest merchant in the village is identified as *familia* by a subordinate individual while the merchant returns the recognition by saying, "Yes, I think he is some family of mine, but I'm not sure how." Even though the majority of Aldeanos can find some degree of kinship with each other, only a limited number of these persons are within the boundaries of kinship that require recognition of reciprocal obligations and sentiments. This recognition does not usually extend collaterally beyond first cousins (*primo hermanos*), although *compadrazgo* relations with cousins beyond this would naturally include them within the effective kinship group. U.S. immigration law strengthens bonds of near kin and helps weaken distant kinship ties.

Even though the cultural ideal is that of dominant masculinity as expressed in *machismo,* family organization is not strictly patrifocal, although one male in a household is accorded the deference of *jefe de la familia*. In some cases, such as a male's absence, lack of economic power, or personal nonaggressiveness, a female can be recognized as both the titular and real *jefe*. Although the most common name in the village is Gómez, the norm of marriage to individuals with previously existing close ties of friendship and common interest, combined with a preference for intrafamilial marriages in order to preserve property holdings, has led to a patrifocality that is more apparent than real.

Ramon, 78, a powerful landowner, maintains four households and has fathered 47 children. Because he assumes both financial and moral responsibility for all these households, he is regarded as *jefe de la familia* and father by all the children. Twenty-two of these children have emigrated to New

York and his home is filled with stacks of formal photographs from children and grandchildren, many signed with statements of affection for *papa* or *abuelo*. Crosscutting economic interests further bind this kindred together both in the Dominican Republic and in New York.

Doña Ana, the moral and civic leader of the community, was born a Pérez, although she is a Gómez through her mother's lineage. Her husband was a first cousin carrying the name Gómez, born and reared in a town some 80 kilometers distant. Since their marriage they have lived in Aldea. She exercises the decision-making power in the family. A house being built with money sent by their New York children is on a site she chose, and the details of construction are ultimately left for her to decide. The house is spoken of as *la casa de doña Ana* or *mi mamá* (the house of doña Ana or my mother), in the community and among her family in New York. The recognition of her leadership within the family is a product of her personal qualities as much as her husband's.

Lottie Gómez de Gómez formed a union with her first cousin but left him behind when she emigrated to New York, where she lived for eighteen years. During her residence in New York she remitted considerable sums of money to purchase land and improve her home. Now retired and drawing a monthly social security check from the U.S., she occupies a position of considerable economic leverage in the area, but does not participate in community social and religious activities. Her house and land are invariably referred to by her name, not that of her husband.

However, other leading figures in the economics of the village, such as Appolo Gómez, a landowner and moneylender, Anton Taváres, the elderly owner of a small *bodega,* and Andreas Gómez, the owner of the largest *almacén,* are all males who are acknowledged to dominate their households. It appears that the focality of a household structure is determined by personal characteristics such as aggressiveness and acquisitiveness, as well as upon the attributes of one's mate.

SOCIAL STRATIFICATION

The population of the village is socially stratified along an economic continuum, the components of which are the possession of the means of production or access to the outputs of this production. Roughly, distinctions are drawn between possession of land or sums of money, those who have regular access to capital through relatives' remittances, those who exist on marginal parcels of land or are *jornaleros* (day laborers), and the unemployed. The former are often referred to as *la gente buena,* the latter as *los pobres.* The position of the intermediate group is far more dependent upon noneconomic factors for its social classification than are the two extremes.

Crosscutting these economic categories is classification based on sentiments and social actions. This is a quality referred to as *confianza,* usually expressed as *una persona de confianza, él tiene confianza.* The attributes of such persons go beyond mere trustworthiness, and may include religious activity or conformity to social norms such as legal marriage and/or conscientious maintenance of one's "outside" family. They are *serio* (proper), willing to help others in crises, without expecting material reciprocation. Thus, most members of the school committee are considered *personas de confianza* because of the hours they devote to working for the new school. Such persons are often referred to as don and doña, marks of respect which are generally accorded older individuals in face-to-face relationships, but applied only to selected individuals when they are not present. Thus, the titles don and doña are terms of address to most older people and to all of those thought of as *la gente buena,* while they are earned terms of reference to those individuals with qualities of *confianza.*

Don Pedro and his wife doña Generosa have lived in the village only since the construction of the dam, but because of their work on community projects, faithful attendance at church, willingness to help solve a variety of personal problems among the poor, they are invariably referred to with the respectful titles of don and doña.*

In a similar manner, doña Ana was accorded great respect. She had for years been chiefly responsible for the upkeep of the church and several individuals in New York named her as the person to whom they owed their education outside the village in Church-operated *colegios.* Even though she had no money to contribute to their education, she had found individuals to support them.

Appolo Gómez, on the other hand, was one of the chief moneylenders and moneychangers in the village. He in no way supported the building of the new school and his daughter lived in an earthen floored *bohío* with her children because he refused to accept her marriage to someone he considered inferior to the family. While he was often addressed as don Polo, especially by those who wished to do business with him, never was such a title used in reference. It is noteworthy that both don Pedro and don Polo occupy their present roles because of the emigration phenomenon. The former is a leader because of the dearth of individuals to fill leadership roles and the latter's wealth is almost entirely based upon money lending and changing connected with the New York exodus.

---

* The social power that don Pedro commands was demonstrated to me once when he and I stood in front of the church and two inebriated young men loudly referred to me as the American Indian who had come to spy upon them (*los indios* was a then-popular term of derision referring to the police). He angrily called to them to shut up and remove their hats. They were offensive to his ears as well as to God in His church. He then commanded them to bow, with hats off, facing the open church door, and ask for forgiveness.

The choice of an individual to be one's *compadre* involves searching for or conferring upon someone the attribute of *confianza*. The acceptance of this relationship carries with it the obligation to act in accordance with the ideal of the concept, at least in this specific relationship. Many instances can be cited in which individuals with public reputations for dishonesty and unfairness act as *compadres* in perfect faith. Indeed, one way of neutralizing potentially threatening individuals is to select them as *compadres*.

The Village School

The *paraje* of Aldea has maintained a publicity operated school for at least 30 years. Until the opening of the 1969 school year classes were held in a dilapidated three-room wooden building; four teachers taught six *cursos*. Morning and afternoon sessions were necessary to accommodate the official enrollment of almost 300. A new eight-classroom building was constructed through the joint efforts of the local population and the national government and dedicated by President Balaguer in the summer of 1969. Designated as a rural district school, it is scheduled to give instruction eventually through grade 8 (intermediate level); so far, lack of teachers has prevented this plan's implementation.

While none of the four teachers meets licensing requirements as rural teachers, the school is more fortunate than most rural schools in that its director, a former seminarian, has at least three years of training beyond his *bachillerato*, plus a year of study in a French-Canadian college. He lacks only the necessary pedagogical courses to meet licensing standards.* Native to the area, he is only distantly related to the chief lineages of the village. He is deeply religious, and a good portion of his time is devoted to serving as lay reader for the novenas said when a priest is not present, conducting *cursillos* of religious nature, and assisting the priest during mass. He intermingles his religious and educational roles freely, so that there is more than the one hour per week of religious instruction prescribed in the curriculum. During Lent, for example, when more masses are held on week days, school was dismissed for the period of the service in which the school director participated. The other teachers and about half the pupils waited in the school or on the playground.

The other three teachers include a nineteen-year old male with a secondary diploma but no training or experience as a teacher, sent

* Unfortunately, in the subsequent school year he left teaching to work with Padre Ricardo in *Acción Social*.

mid-year to replace a teacher described by the school inspector as "mad," and two females who each had two years of teaching experience but were more than a year short of completing their secondary training. All three lived near Santiago and were in the village only on school days; their interaction with the community was minimal.

The teachers were critical of the results of their labor, fixing the blame on lack of textbooks, lack of interest on the part of students, and the lack of parental support due to the parent's being in New York. They blamed their reliance on rote learning on the lack of materials. Community leaders, however, criticized teachers, blaming the teachers' difficulties on insufficient academic preparation and limited interest in the work. Each child is expected to purchase his own textbooks which cost, depending upon the grade, as much as six dollars per child. The second-grade teacher claimed that not more than two pupils owned all the required books; in the sixth grade almost everyone had the required texts. After two months in the school, the 19-year-old male teacher bitterly observed, "What we do has not even five cents value. This is often worse than no education," as we watched one of the other teachers put a story on the blackboard for her class to copy. It contained a variety of spelling and grammatical errors.

TABLE 4. SCHOOL REGISTRATION IN ALDEA, FEBRUARY 1969

Grade	Officially Registered	Unregistered but Attending
1	120	16
2	28	
3	36	
4	40	2
5	40	3
6	14	

Note: The unregistered category is the result of official limitations on class size; additional students can be accommodated only by allowing them to attend school unregistered.

The disproportionately large number of children in grade one is partly the effect of early dropouts, and even more the result of the relatively rigorous standards of achievement required for promotion to grade two. At the end of the first year pupils are expected to have mastered the rudiments of reading and writing (copying) skills, and begun basic arithmetic. Until this is achieved, the child is retained. As a result, it is not unusual for a child to repeat grade one several times. In this particular school, there is one first-grade class composed only of repeaters; one thirteen-year-old boy was repeating for the fifth time.

While most the eligible younger children in the village are enrolled in school, their attendance is often irregular. Although parents may make considerable effort to provide schooling for their children, other activities occupy a higher priority than does actual school attendance. Don Pedro, the president of the *Padres y Amigos de la Escuela*, who devoted a great deal of time to building the new school, regularly kept his 14-year-old daughter at home to guard the premises whenever both he and his wife expected to be away. Water-hauling responsibilities delegated to younger children in households living beyond the central water supply lines also keep some students from attending school at times.

Even if a child learns how to read in school, there are almost no opportunities to read outside school. The only periodical available locally is the Monday morning edition of *El Caribe,* a Santo Domingo newspaper, which publishes the entire list of numbers in the weekly national lottery drawn on Sundays. The only household apparently containing any reading materials during my stay in Aldea was don Pedro's; he had a small bookshelf of materials received when he and his wife enrolled in an international correspondence school. In most households members are called upon to exercise their reading skills only when letters from New York correspondents arrive. Eighty-eight percent of the household have radios; there are nine television sets in the village, though reception is limited by the distance from Santiago and the mountainous terrain.

EFFECT OF MIGRATION ON THE SCHOOL

The impact of migration upon the school has been felt in a number of ways. Traditionally, the school's authority has been maintained through its position as an extension of parental authority. Aldeanos speak of the teacher as being the "father in the classroom." Physical punishment is all but unknown since the teacher relies heavily upon sanctions for misbehavior to come from within the culprit's household. However, the teachers complain that this relationship has been upset because so many children are left behind with one parent, grandparents, distant kinsmen, or friends, by parents who have gone to New York. These individuals often lack either the authority or the ability to discipline the child left in their care.

Bernice was left in the village to care for her four younger children while her husband and three older children migrated to New York. She has held a residence visa for a number of years and was applying for visas for the remaining children without success. The boys were attentive to their mother but skipped school. She was aware of this but felt that without the strong hand of her husband she was helpless in disciplining them. After waiting over a year for the children's visas to no avail, it was essential that she go to New York herself in order not to lose her own visa. The boys were left in the care of a friend and when I met her again in New York, she was full of tales of woe about problems being created by her boys in the village. "They tell me that they are acting like *tigres* [juvenile delinquents]."

Migration to New York affects teacher supply also. In the course of field work in New York, I met several dozen former teachers including four who had formerly been teaching in Aldea. One of the feeder schools was closed for almost a month during the school year because the teacher migrated to New York and no one could be found to replace her.

The 12-year old son of Andreas Gómez, the chief merchant in the town, had been enrolled in a private school in Santiago when the family first returned from the United States, but the arrangement was found to be awkward and expensive. He was then sent to the village school, even though the parents were aware of the inferior quality of the education there. "He already knows how to read and write. It's more important that my American learn how to be a Dominican," reasoned the father.

In addition, the almost universal assumption, especially among older children, is that one day they will go to New York themselves. This tends to create an indifferent attitude toward what goes on in the school. They are well aware of the vast numbers who have gone to New York as illiterates and have, from the Aldeano point of view, been successful, that is, gained employment and acquired seemingly large sums of capital. They see little value in a Dominican education in Spanish which has nothing to do with the life they intend to lead in New York. By the same token, at least a few have concluded that the kind of jobs held by those in New York with considerable education by Dominican standards is not significantly different than those with poorer education.

It would be highly inaccurate to ascribe any common attitude toward the utility of a formal education to the villagers. As might be expected, differential reactions are based upon individual experience in attending school, as well as on attitudes received through the socialization process within the family and peer group. School and attendance at school are almost universally acknowledged as a good thing. However, a dichotomy exists between those who consider formal education instrumental in achieving economic and social mobility and those who hope to achieve fulfillment through other means for themselves and for their children. Thus, there are those who are willing to sacrifice in order to achieve schooling and those who opt for employment at the earliest opportunity. For many, school is a "holding operation" until the time some other social or occupational role becomes available: marriage or motherhood, employment, or migration to the United States.

For many the personal experience in school has been negative. The nature and quality of instruction even for an eager pupil is limited; for the less gifted or motivated pupil it can be devastating. The experience of failure is frequent, as illustrated by the high numbers of repeating pupils at all levels throughout the Republic. In Aldea the holding power of the school is undoubtedly greater because many school-aged children are supported by remittances and alternate activities are limited.

In the past one way for an individual in the village to acquire more schooling than was locally available was to attend a Church-operated boarding school. Very often such an institution assumed the student was being educated for a vocation within the Church. Padre Ricardo and the school director are examples of this. The number of people interviewed in New York who had had all or part of their schooling under such circumstances, but who dropped out prior to making final commitments to religious vocations, indicates that religious concerns motivated them far less than their desire for more schooling. I knew of only two adolescents from the village who were currently enrolled in such schools. One reason for this shift undoubtedly is that migration to New York has been substituted for education as an avenue for upward social and economic mobility.

The school is, of course, one of the societal elements contributing to the world view carried by the emigrants to New York. Through the specific example of the school it is possible to demonstrate the change taking place as a result of out-migration in a number of social institutions of the home society. In addition, the outlook the immigrant brings with him to New York has important repercussions in the way he will use institutions of the new environment in his eventual accommodation to life in New York.

CHAPTER THREE

Interaction: The Village and New York City

Communication with New York

About half the 150 to 200 pieces of letter mail arriving daily in Aldea originate in the United States, almost all of them in New York. Of this number about 35 are received as registered mail. Letters are registered because they contain remittances, usually in the form of money orders. Many individuals do not trust the public postal system and there are frequent rumors about the disappearance and pilferage of mail. The *agente de correo* (postmaster) protested these rumors to me, assuming they suggested that he was dishonest. However, letters appear from time to time in both New York and Dominican publications alleging robbery of the mails, and occasional news articles note arrests for mail pilferage. Post offices in heavily Hispanic areas of New York City display signs indicating that registered mail to the Dominican Republic cannot be assured delivery and should never contain checks, money orders, or cash.

Public service mail is only a minor element of the communication process between New York and the Dominican Republic. Individuals arriving and departing daily between New York and Aldea bear vast numbers of messages, some written, some oral. Almost any individual who returns from New York comes laden with messages, gifts, and money from New York residents. By the same token, anyone leaving for New York carries such gifts as a packet of Dominican candy or a bottle of rum, as well as messages for New Yorkers. New York-bound money may be house rent to an owner living in New York, or for purchasing merchandise that will be sent back by another bearer.

New York residents, especially the more sophisticated, sometimes express resentment at being cast into this time-consuming bearer role, but few seem to refuse. In fact, most welcome the structural position in which such a role places them and are not averse to seeking out this role. Being asked to transport as much as $4,000 to $6,000 of other people's money is proof of *confianza*. In addition, the bearer then has legitimate reason to call upon and enter the households of a wider variety of individuals when he arrives back in the Republic. The returnee, who already holds considerable status because of his residence in New York and consequent assumed experience and affluence, is able to expand his reputation through personal contact.

Bernice lives with her four sons in Aldea while her husband and three older children live in New York. Two days after arriving for a holiday after an absence of almost four years, Ramon, a New York resident, appeared at her door in Aldea. After she had vouched for my integrity, he removed a pack of letters from his pocket and pulled out one addressed to her. He then took from another pocket a very large roll of U.S. $20 bills and after consulting a list of names and figures, he counted out six bills for Bernice. For the next hour we sat and talked of life in New York and of Bernice's immediate and extended family there. He told where her husband was now employed and about her family's new apartment in New York and recent encounters with Aldeanos *allá*. Talk turned to a new restaurant in Queens opened by an Aldeano, and to a knife fight that had taken place on Mott Street between two Aldeanos over the alleged refusal of one to repay a debt to the other. Bernice commented on Ramon's spotless and freshly pressed shirt and trousers and brightly shined shoes. This provided him the opening to tell of his own life in New York. He dwelt on the positive aspects of life there, the furniture for his new apartment and, most of all, his automobile. After his departure the letter was opened and read aloud by the mother to her boys who in turn read and reread it after she was finished. It was written by a son and daughter because the husband was illiterate. Neither of the writers had been long in school, one never passed beyond grade one, and the letter was not lengthy. It consisted of expressions of love, concern about the heavy snow that had just fallen in New York, and an admonition to the boys to do nothing to dishonor their mother and family name. Each son was to receive a specific sum as spending money from the total remittance.

Other letters from New York residents contained family information—births, marriages, comments on recent events in the village that the writer had heard about. Often the letters would contain instructions about the status of requests for visas. From the letters and from the comments of the returnees, one would gain only positive impressions of life in New York. This lack of balance in the reports is reflected in the developing expectations of recruits to the migrant stream, as well as in the expectations of family members remaining in Aldea about the ability of those *allá* to send support money.

One of the school teachers who was called upon to read a number of letters for illiterate recipients commented, "Usually the first letters from New York express sadness and loneliness and discomfort from the weather. The regimentation of factory hours and daily work is a new thing for them. But very quickly they stop writing that. Especially after their first pay check and they only tell things which make the young people think the streets there are made with gold."

REMITTANCES

The almost complete dependence of the population of Aldea on money remitted from the United States must be emphasized.* Aside from positions as government workers—mechanics and laborers at the dam, the police detachment guarding it, the two post office employees and four school teachers—there is almost no employment for those without land. Those *jornaleros* who find irregular agricultural or construction work earn one *peso* per day plus a meal. Most of the land is held by a few individuals who seldom recruit workers outside their own immediate kin group. Other land is held by and large in smaller-than-subsistence plots and provides almost no opportunity for employment. The sale of surplus products from these holdings generates little cash.

It is impossible to estimate the amount of money coming into Aldea from New York. An officially pegged rate of exchange, coupled with import laws that place a premium on foreign currency, has led to an institutionalized black market for foreign funds. In the major cities of the Dominican Republic, the premium fluctuates between ten and fifteen percent, depending on seasonal demands for foreign goods and consequent need for foreign exchange. Before Christmas and Mother's Day, two traditional gift-giving days, the demand for foreign-made consumer goods is highest. The black market functions openly, with some brokers maintaining fixed offices known to everyone. According to banking officers in Santiago, arrests are made only when individuals hustle directly in the post office building in their eagerness to bid for checks. One officer in the Banco Central estimated unofficially that more than $12,000,000 annually was remitted to the Dominican Republic by U.S. residents. The difficulty of estimating is compounded by the fact that many individuals have demand deposit bank accounts in the United States; amounts withdrawn from these accounts and carried to the Dominican Republic do not appear on any balance of payments for the nation as a whole.

In the village the exchange rate is usually one percent lower than the rate in the cities. Four individuals are active money changers. One

---

* One of the local money changers had lived for a number of years in New York. During the flurry of one particularly busy day of exchange activities he held up a large number of checks and money orders from the U.S. and began to sing in English, "God Bless America."

of them, a storekeeper, claims to average slightly more than $2,000 each week in such transactions. However, in one week just before Christmas, he changed $6,000. His profits came not from the exchange itself, but through the charge accounts of households dependent upon remittances. The majority of his accounts were based upon the knowledge that one or more individuals in New York were contributing regularly to maintenance of a household in Aldea. Of the 146 households about which such information was obtained, some 60 percent were dependent in varying degrees on remittances from New York. This dependence ranged from complete reliance on monthly checks to receiving only irregularly sent sums.

TABLE 5. HOUSEHOLD RELATIONSHIP TO NEW YORK KINSMEN

	No.	%
With immediate family in New York	123	65
No kinsmen in U.S.	15	10
Persons residing in household with U.S. visa	40	27
Receiving remittances	87	60
N = 46		

Three examples of varying circumstances under which remittances are sent are:

Lucy lives in Aldea with six of her children. Her husband and four older children live in New York and together they regularly send her $150 a month. Both she and the *almacén* owner estimate that she charges about $100 monthly to her account with him. She is obliged to cash the remittance checks in the store because of the arrangement.

Andreas maintains a small *bodega* adjoining his neat, well-kept home. He has seventeen children living in New York. He himself lived for three years in New York, saved his money to repay large debts incurred in raising his large family, then returned and reopened his store. The store and the production of a few *tareas* of agricultural land provide him a relatively comfortable rural living. His children send money for such amenities as his television set. Both he and his wife maintain their U.S. residence visas by making annual trips to New York. The cost of these trips is met by various children pooling funds to purchase the plane tickets.

Gracela, is a fifteen-year-old unwed mother. The father of her year-old child remits $15 per month "for the baby's milk." She expresses hope that he may marry her and take them both to New York. An interview in New York with him indicates that he has no such intention, although he accepts responsibility for the child.

Recipients and would-be recipients consider remittances an obligation of their more fortunate relatives. They also consider it the right of those remaining in the Republic to receive this kind of assistance. Many of the younger ones assume that eventually they too will go *allá*, and that they in turn will accept the obligation to send remittances, or to become part of some unit of mutual economic assistance in New York. Not all accept the obligation, but the sanctions are powerful, and it is the norm of the community that such help will be forthcoming. Gossip provides considerable leverage to influence those who do not meet such standards.

Fausto failed to provide for his wife and four children who remained in Aldea, while it was common knowledge that he drank and gambled heavily in New York. The burden of his wife's care fell upon members of his family who had remained in the Republic. They in turn pressured him through their linkages to other members of the *pariente* in New York to remind him of his obligations to "the family name." One informant living next door to Fausto's sister in New York told of a terrible shouting match during which she berated Fausto for the shame he brought to her. Apparently the drinking and gambling were not criticized in themselves; only Fausto's failure to meet his obligations to his legal wife and their children came under attack.

Returnees

A typical outbound *carro público* (taxi) leaving Aldea for Santo Domingo and the airport might contain four passengers headed for the airport and one or more others going to the United States Consulate for interviews concerning the acquisition of a visa. In the winter months the traffic is heavier and as many as five vehicles are available for the journey. On a single day in December 1968 it was reported that 46 natives of the Aldea area arrived during the pre-Christmas rush.*

Públicos direct to Aldea from the airport are more expensive than alternate methods, which involve changing cars in the city of Santo Domingo and then again in Santiago. Such alternatives are far more time consuming and less prestigious than to arrive or depart in the direct *públicos*. The *públicos* are well kept, late-model American cars, while the route taxis from Santiago are usually small European cars, often in poor condition. The direct-line drivers announce their return

---

* Mid-December until early April is the optimal visiting period; the important religious holidays coincide with the cold weather in New York. This is also an active agricultural period, and Aldeanos who are trying to maintain their small *terrenos* while also working in New York come to the village at this time, when they can. However, since many of the New York factories in which the migrants work are closed for annual vacations in July and August, some people can come home only during this period.

in the late afternoon with loud horn-blowing at the outskirts of the village; as they drive down the street everyone in the village is alerted to the arriving returnees. Usually the driver will deliver his passengers to the doors of the houses for which they are destined, indicating to the village at large which houses are hosting returnees. My March 1969 household census indicated that 36 people were then in the village as temporary visitors from New York; this numbers shifts from day to day.

The behavior of the newly arrived returnees has become predictable, reflecting their perception of how to act in a particular role, in response to the expectations of family and friends. Their most obvious expressions of success are the style and quality of clothing, bought in New York. Clothing throughout the Dominican Republic is generally similar to that worn in the United States during warm weather. Working-class males usually wear a cotton shirt and lightweight trousers; women wear cotton or synthetic dresses. For the poor and the *campesino* the basic standard is the same, but the degree of wear is greater. The well-dressed New York male arrives in Aldea, only hours out of Kennedy airport, wearing a suit, white shirt, and tie; a woman wears a dressy dress or suit, stockings, and has an elaborate coiffure. During the entire visit, attire is impeccable, although dressed-up traveling clothes are changed for more comfortable lightweight garments. One former New York resident who has since returned to Aldea permanently commented about a visiting uncle, "Now he needs a clean shirt every day. I knew him in New York. I know how he lives there. There he wears the same shirt all week long."

Both men and women carry much luggage, laden with gifts and articles to be sold or traded, usually clothing and such small appliances as radios, blenders, and portable phonographs. The days following arrival are spent in a round of visits during which gifts and remittances are distributed. Business transactions are also conducted.

The returnee aims to impress villagers with his affluence. In a drinking session he is expected to pay the bill. Small children hang about when he walks outside, hoping he will give them coins or buy them a sweet. Attendance at Sunday morning mass provides additional opportunities to display affluence; in the collection plate any contribution larger than small coins is certain to have been deposited by a visiting New York resident.

Younger male returnees can usually be found among the young unemployed group who gather in the street in front of the shops, in the building housing two pool tables, and in the one sporadically opened local bar. It is not unusual to find a small group of local youths being hosted on an extended spree by a younger returnee. The spree may include not only the consumption of liberal quantities of beer or rum, but the hiring of one of the *públicos* as the group's personal car for a drunken journey about the countryside, concluding with a visit to a prostitute in Santiago.

In most of these contacts the conversations and actions of the visitors are aimed at and result in the appearance of a worldly, sophisticated, and affluent individual.* Life in New York is repeatedly described, reports given on the kind of automobile a recent migrant to New York has obtained, or the furniture and appliances that someone else, undoubtedly a kinsman of some of those listening, has just bought. Other topics of conversation include the prices of goods in New York stores and opportunities for obtaining work *allá*. Time is also spent discussing the various ways of gaining U.S. visas, or circumventing immigration laws. All this, exaggerated or distorted as it may be, helps prepare the potential migrant—especially the adolescent who is literally waiting his turn to go north—for life in New York.

PERMANENT RETURNEES

A number of individuals who spent considerable time in New York have returned to Aldea after accumulating sufficient capital or other resources to live more luxuriously than they would have done otherwise. They serve as everyday models for actual and potential migrants, and are ever-present examples of what can be achieved by going to New York, no matter how painful the process of leaving familiar surroundings may be. So far only a small percentage of the migrants actually have returned to Aldea permanently, one reason being that the period of this migration has been too short for many to have made good and come home already. However, most migrants expect to return eventually. Among Aldeanos any discussion about leaving for New York implicitly assumes the move to be only temporary, with permanent return the ultimate goal.

Not all returnees are to be found in the village. A number live in Santo Domingo, and even more in Santiago, where more of the amenities of urban life with which living in New York acquainted them can be found than in Aldea.

Two successful returnees who live in the village are described here.

* This desire to be perceived as successful is part of a change in self perception that migration usually triggers. This change was most succintly summed up by the schoolmaster's remark, "Yes, they do change. It's as if they are no longer asleep." The ability to speak English is an overt marker of change. Frequently the returnees insisted upon speaking English with me in public no matter how limited their skills might be. In more private encounters we spoke exclusively in Spanish.

Lulu, aged 70, is the oldest returned immigrant. She lived for almost 20 years in New York, working as a machine operator in a clothing factory, and draws a monthly U.S. social security retirement check. During her stay in New York Lulu saved money, and together with her consensual husband, a man much older than she who had remained in the village, she purchased land offered for sale by individuals needing money for the passage to New York. Her house, on one side of the town park, is large and well-kept, filled with furniture and appliances brought from the United States. Two of her husband's sons live in New York. She claims to have made more than 20 round trips between New York and Aldea in her lifetime; her first trip, prior to the time of direct Santo Domingo-to-New York flights, took three days.

Andreas, aged 35, is the most important store owner in the village. He spent nearly ten years working in New York. His wife, Maria, is a first cousin he came to know in New York. Although she was born in the village, she was taken to New York as a youngster by her mother when her parents were divorced; her mother was not from the immediate area and is not a member of any of the few kindred groups of Aldea. They were married twelve years ago and worked hard to save money to return to the village. Andreas and his wife built a house, the most modern in the area and the only private dwelling with an indoor bathroom, on land adjacent to her father's house, which is the oldest in the village. Husband and wife both have siblings in New York as well as in Aldea. During her annual two-month trip to New York, necessary to retain her U.S. residence visa, she visits her mother and brothers there. During this New York period she returns to her former job as a factory worker, and proudly speaks of *her* money as opposed to that of her husband. The couple has three children, a 12-year-old son born in New York, often referred to as "our American," and two younger sons born in the Republic.

Although such individuals are perceived as models of success, they are not solely responsible for their achievements. Success is dependent upon a network of familial relationships and alliances in New York and the Dominican Republic. Lulu's husband, for example, remained in the village during her long absence, caring for her interests there. Today his two sons, whose migration to New York Lulu arranged, help maintain linkages to a New York network and keep watch over her financial interests (loans made to other migrants) there. Although they themselves do not indicate an interest in returning at this time, the house and land in Aldea will be theirs.

Similarly, the marriage of Andreas and Maria linked two important Aldean families, even though it took place in New York. In discussing marital patterns and the frequency of *primo hermano* (first cousin) marriages, informants frequently used this union as an example of marriage which served to preserve assets and land within the family. Andreas and Maria themselves said their marriage stemmed from the close-knit network in New York of which they were a part. Andreas has decided to allow his U.S. residence visa to expire because an annual journey to New York would disrupt his business. However, in addition to Maria's continued linkage to New York, Andreas' parents frequently visit their children in New York, providing contact with people and events there. For example, Andreas arranged for the purchase as an investment of a house in Santiago for a brother-in-law now living in New York. In turn his *almacén* extends credit based upon expected New York remittances which can be collected, if necessary, by his New York kinsmen. The frequent traffic of family members between New York and the Republic allows for an almost instantaneous mail-order service of personal articles as well as business items. Maria bought a small adding machine for use in the store when she arrived in New York for her annual northern pilgrimage, and it was brought back within days by Andreas' father who was returning home.

There is a former New Yorker who provides a rare negative example of what can happen to villagers in the city. A half-crazed herdsman, whose only companions are his three cows with whom he is in constant conversation, he lived for several years in New York, and according to local legend worked hard to save a "fortune." He formed a union with a woman, some say a Puerto Rican, though others think she was from Santo Domingo, who fleeced him of every penny of his savings. The loss of his hard-won money unbalanced him, and he returned to the only things he could trust, a bit of land and his cattle.

One result of the stream of returnees, both temporary and permanent, and the consequent dissemination of information about the United States is that the potential for emigration increases. After little more than 20 years of out-migration the ideal life cycle of the majority of the village population has come to include some time spent in the United States. All young males interviewed assumed that one day they would go to New York to earn their fortunes and then to return to the Dominican Republic to live a comfortable life based upon their savings. Returnees represent concrete proof to the villagers of the feasibility and desirability of becoming part of the migrant stream.

Not only are the returnees important in encouraging migration, but they are instrumental in conditioning expectations. The migrant arriving in New York is aware of much that he will experience; he also has some misinformation, the result of deliberate distortion by the informant. For example, in discussing his weekly salary, the New Yorker visiting Aldea may not mention the considerable difference between gross and net (*limpio,* literally "clean") income in the United States. He might inflate the amount of his savings or cover up his feelings about the rigidity and constraints on individual freedom that are created by factory employment.

Even if the informant attempts to describe completely his life in New York, another kind of distortion results from the gaps between what the informant describes and the experience of his listeners. A visitor describing his job as an elevator operator finds it difficult to communicate what he does to an individual who has never been in a building higher than two stories and surely has never seen an elevator. An interview with one family was interrupted by the arrival of a *compadre* from New York who in the course of the conversation described his factory job, which required that he operate a plastic-molding machine. The technology of agriculture in this part of the Republic is rudimentary; the *machete*, a long-bladed knife, is an all-purpose tool, serving as both a shovel and hoe. On most small hillside plots no other tool is used in farming. On this family's small isolated *parcela*, a systematic search of the technology employed revealed that the wheel was not used in any observable form in either the house or the field. The *compadre* had with him a transistor radio, and together we listened to a Voice of America broadcast of the Apollo 9 splashdown. The ensuing conversation revealed not even a rudimentary knowledge of the solar system on the part of the *campesino*, and a very fragmentary understanding on the part of the supposedly sophisticated New York *compadre*. But the *campesino* sitting in his earthern-floored thatched house listening to his well-dressed kinsman describe life in New York had every reason to believe that, indeed, New York offered an opportunity to escape from his own subsistence-level existence. Even if the visitor were to communicate the difficulties of life in New York, it would be difficult to argue realistically that migration to New York would not materially enhance the migrant's position.

Poverty is always relative. From the point of view of many Americans, most Dominican immigrants exist at a marginal level in New York. Even though the most economically or socially depressed segment of the Dominican population is seldom able to marshal the necessary resources for the trip north, those who go have an opportunity to improve their living standards considerably. Mangin (1970: xxviii) points out in an overview of anthropological studies of peasant migration to cities that there is a recurrent theme in such studies in the South American context. "The conditions are often so oppressive [in the rural areas], that migrants to urban areas, although appearing to be in an appalling economic state, are often pleased with the relative improvement in their status." Thus, continuous contact with New York residents serves to accentuate for Aldeanos the relative material advantages available for those living *allá*.

PART II

TRANSITION

THE TRIBUTARIO: *Smooths the way to the United States for many Dominicans.*

CHAPTER FOUR

The Migration Process

So far we have examined the home village and seen how emigration has had fundamental effects upon culture and society there. Of great import is the fact that out-migration has resulted in patterns of behavior which precondition the potential New Yorker for his expected life *allá*. Before presenting an analysis of the New York segment of the immigrants' social field, we examine the process of gaining entry into the United States, particularly the difficulties involved in acquiring a visa. The impact of U.S. immigration law on social behavior, both in the receiving and the sending societies, can only be appreciated through a detailed examination of the process of obtaining either legal or illegal entrance into the United States.

The Law

Requirements pertaining to immigration have become much more complex since 1924, when the first laws to constrict the flow of immigrants into the United States became effective. The entry of any foreign citizen into the United States is now governed by a highly complicated set of laws, regulations, and administrative and judicial decisions.* This complexity, in combination with the functional illiteracy and distrust of officialdom of many Dominicans, leads to the creation of a whole system of social relationships, values, and beliefs about obtaining a visa and migrating to the U.S. These behavioral patterns are based not only on the reality of the immigration process as systematically spelled out by law, regulation, and practice, but also on what Gonzales (1971) has called a folklore concerning the process.

The intent of the immigration and nationality acts as applied to

* A legal textbook on U.S. immigration law indicates the difficulties when it points out to the student that "These immigration statutes are intricate and complex. They must be carefully consulted on each immigration problem to avoid error. *It may never be assumed that the statute will contain a certain provision because logic so dictates*" [italics mine] (Wildes 1968:26).

Dominicans is fairly simple to outline, despite the complexity of their implementation. Basically the law defines two classes of entrant: those who wish to come for short periods of time for the primary purpose of visiting or for specific periods of education; and those who desire to remain for longer periods of time and perhaps eventually to exercise the option of applying for United States citizenship. Thus, entry permits or visas fall into two basic categories: immigrant (sometimes called residence) and nonimmigrant (tourist and student) visas. From the point of view of the potential migrant the basic difference is that the nonimmigrant visa is valid only for a stated period of time and under it employment for remuneration is normally forbidden. U.S. citizenship can be obtained only through an immigrant visa. The immigrant visa is normally valid indefinitely and with it an individual obtains the right to work remuneratively as well as to participate in almost all governmental functions with equal rights of a citizen; a nonimmigrant cannot legally receive social welfare benefits. Thus, migrants are better off with immigrant visas, but many Dominicans, especially less sophisticated ones from the rural areas, do not understand the distinction. Mere entrance into the U.S. is all they desire, and the technicalities are unimportant. Few Dominican immigrants who are eligible become citizens. The impact of the 1968 Act * is yet to be felt in full, but since it places additional premiums on citizenship vis-a-vis alien residency, undoubtedly a great number of immigrants will apply.

Normally, obtaining a visitor's visa to the U.S. is not difficult for citizens of foreign countries. In most countries it is obtained by filling out a card containing fourteen simple identifying questions and presenting this to an American Consular official for on-the-spot approval. However, acquiring a U.S. residence visa is far more complicated and involves the presentation of quantities of validated documents, followed by long delays. Broadly speaking, since 1968 individuals from Western Hemisphere nations have been eligible for residence visas if they were either dependent spouses, minor children, or parents of persons already citizens or possessors of immigrant visas, or could present evidence that they are candidates for employment based upon evidence of Labor Certification.

The intricacies of the law have led to offices within United States governmental bureaucracies to deal with the disposition of visa appli-

* In July 1968 the immigration and naturalization law was altered in basic ways, especially pertaining to citizens from countries of the Western Hemisphere. Since this research was conducted in the period immediately following this change in the law, there may be a seeming contradiction between present requirements and statements made here. Most of the persons with whom this study dealt in New York had entered the U.S. under the previous law.

cations, and also to third parties who assist individuals in applying for visas. The practice of immigration law is a recognized and profitable segment of the legal profession.* But only some visa "specialists" have legal training. Visa brokers ** manifest themselves in a variety of other forms: as tourist agents, money lenders, or straightforwardly as solicitors of visas. " 'After the sugar industry hustling visas has become the biggest business there is in the Dominican Republic,' said one lawyer, only half in jest" (*The New York Times*, May 15, 1970). The role of *tributario* or *corredor* (essentially a broker) is a common one, operating in conjunction with most government offices in the Dominican Republic.*** Individuals applying for visas, combining their own experience of dealing with bureaucracy with the very real complexity of U.S. immigration processes, actively seek out individuals to occupy this role of broker.

The broker role may also be played by a New York kinsman who is willing and able to find a prospective employer, or is able to complete the required forms in English, and understand the labyrinth of bureaucracy, having passed through it himself. Since he is the one most likely to have access to the cash necessary to pay a professional broker, as well as to pay for transportation, the role he occupies is often more akin to that of patron than of broker. The openness in which the professional operates is demonstrated in advertisements, appearing in both Dominican and New York Spanish-language newspapers, offering to help find jobs and visas. At least one large legal firm specializing in immigration law maintains offices in Santo Domingo and New York.

But the complex law leads to much subterfuge and deception. What, for example, distinguishes a master tailor from a sewing machine operator? What constitutes mental retardation which could exclude a dependent child? It is the visa broker who, based upon his knowledge of the law and experience with its implementation, is best qualified to tell the applicant how an application should be directed

* The Association of Immigration and Nationality Lawyers has a suggested minimum fee schedule ranging from $50 for the simplest kind of request to $2500 for a Supreme Court Review. "The suggested minimum fees do not take into account the ability of the client to pay" (AINL).

** We here follow the distinctions made by Mayer in pointing out that a *patron* recruits followers by his power to disperse his favors. The *broker* is a middleman attracting followers who believe him able to influence the person who controls the favors. A given individual may occupy both roles (Mayer 1967).

*** It was necessary for me to apply for a *cedula*, or identification card, because of my extended residence in the Republic. Next to the *Dirección de la Cedula* in Santiago is a small office opening on to the street with a large sign *Diligencia en cedula, pasaporte, Fototaticas* (sic) *Documentos en general* (help in obtaining cedulas, etc.). For a payment of 50¢ the *tributario* filled out the necessary form for me and then escorted me past waiting lines in the *Dirección* into the inner office of the director where the application was handled expeditiously. What part of the fee was handed over to the official is not known, but my Dominican informants assumed he received something.

and handled. An application need not be based upon deception, but the fine line between truth and fiction is often not clear. Embroidery of an individual's work experience may determine his case. Sometimes clear fraud is committed. The falsification of a birth certificate for a 23-year-old in order to qualify as a 19-year-old dependent is one such example. An open market exists for marriages between persons in New York and those seeking to get there.

Prior to 1968 there was no numerical limitation on citizens from Western Hemisphere nations. That is, as many as applied who met the basic requirements of dependency or occupation could obtain immigration visas and enter the U.S. Under Public Law 89-236 which became fully implemented in July of 1968, an annual ceiling of 120,000 was effected for natives of the Western Hemisphere. The full import of this quota did not become apparent until two years later. Formerly, an individual from the Dominican Republic who met all the requirements could expect a waiting time of one to three months from the time complete applications had been accepted until the granting of an immigration visa. By 1970, however, the delay was fifteen months, as the applicants awaited the availability of an assigned quota number (INS 1971–72). Contributing to the delay is the fact that the arbitrary number of 120,000 is below the annual total number of immigrants from these areas in years immediately preceding 1968. A further complicating factor is the necessity of using numbers from the limited pool to adjust the almost half million Cuban refugees to permanent residence (immigrant) status. The delays resulting from this new set of ground rules affects not only prospective Dominican immigrants, but all Latin Americans as well as Canadians and the West Indians.

Tremendous pressures are building in the sending societies as the backlog grows. The pressures and frustrations of attempting to bring other family members into the U.S. are also felt by the immigrants already in New York. As long as unemployment remains high within the sending society, the pressures to enter the United States legally or illegally will continue. At the same time any improvement in the Republic's economic situation would serve to stimulate emigration as more individuals obtained sufficient resources to exit the country. Two effects of the law already discernible are the increase in the numbers of violators of visitors' visas and the increase in the number of Dominican nationals seeking U.S. citizenship. From 1967 to 1971, an increase of 230 percent in the number of such persons naturalized took place (INS 1971). It is the estimate of the American Consul in Santo Domingo that at least 500,000 Dominican citizens could be expected to emigrate to the U.S. within ten years if the arbitrary numerical restriction were lifted.

The Meaning of a Visa

In the Dominican Republic the acquisition of a valid immigrant visa, and, to a lesser extent, a tourist nonimmigrant visa, has come to have cultural valuations not intended by the issuing country. Not only is it a formalized acknowledgement that the holder possesses certain minimal prerequisites, but for some politically oriented individuals it represents an escape hatch in case of difficulties. The need to leave the country is not necessarily confined to periods of great national crisis; it may also be necessary for individuals whose private political fortunes are suddenly endangered.

A visa has also come to be an attestation of the possessor's political and moral righteousness. In spite of often bitter criticism of *los yanquis,* the fear of Communism in the Dominican Republic is great, and it is universally acknowledged that the North Americans will not grant visas to known Communists. In much the same way persons of ill-repute will not be issued a visa. For example, the owner of one large hotel in Santo Domingo cannot be issued a visa by the U.S. Consul because it is widely known that his hotel is a house of prostitution. This seeming paradox of using the "imperialist Americans" as arbiters, genuinely removed from local political machinations, is typical of the vacillation and dependence of the Dominican Republic in most of its relations with the United States.

These additional advantages of a visa have relatively little meaning for the immigrant from Aldea, or for the vast majority of the rural folk migrating to New York. But universally the mere possession of a valid visa represents economic power both potential and immediate. It is potential in that the individual has access to New York employment, and its supposedly high wages. It has immediate economic value in that credit will be granted to the individual on the basis of his potential. "A guy with a visa can have any girl in town. Someone will always loan him money because they know he can pay it back when he goes up there. A visa is really worth money," said a leading Aldeano merchant. In addition, possession of a visa imputes social status to its possessor independent of other attributes. Much as money takes on values above and beyond its instrumental value, the U.S. visa is sought after by many who have no immediate intention of leaving the country.

Obtaining a Visa

On any given work day the American Consulate in Santo Domingo processes from 400 to 600 applications for immigrant and nonimmigrant visas.* Hours before the offices open, a waiting line begins to form. The consulate, a building left over from the World Fair of 1954, the *Feria de la Paz y Confraternidad del Mundo Libre,* a Trujillo fiasco, is too small to provide enough offices to handle traffic, or to provide seating for the waiting throng. Consequently, an outdoor shaded area containing long rows of backless benches is provided. Those without seats are forced to stand in the tropical sun or seek shelter in nearby buildings during the not infrequent rainstorms. Anyone familiar with a typical aggregation of the same number of Dominicans under other circumstances would be struck by the almost absolute silence of the waiting throng. Noteworthy also is the exemplary dress of almost everyone, rustic country men often uncomfortably clad in coats and ties. The silence is broken by the periodic calling of a name over the loudspeaker system. Rare outbursts of temper as an individual attempts to get out of place in line may provoke a moment of noise but this is quickly hushed by the surrounding crowd.

The group at the consulate is made up of those seeking information and blank forms; those called by the consular officials for preliminary examination or final determination of their applications for immigrant visas; and, by far the largest group, those applying for tourist visas. The two doors leading into the consulate, one marked for U.S. citizens only, are guarded by members of the National Police. Dominican information seekers never enter the building, and are handled by a Dominican employee of the consulate through a window booth. Persons awaiting visa approval wait to be summoned one by one over the loudspeaker.

At the edges of the consulate grounds, the activity of the street takes over: vendors hawking various foods and *buscones* (solicitors) soliciting riders for the cars returning to the center of the city. Small groups of people stand talking, sometimes glancing up furtively to see if anyone is observing their activities; these groups may merely be conversing, but often in their midst will be individuals (*buscones,* or *tributarios*) carrying on business: offering advice, for a price, on how best to apply for a visa; selling blank application forms that are available free at the consulate; or perhaps coaching a client who is scheduled for an interview. Never do these activities openly trespass upon consular property. There is tension in the air. For many in the crowd it is the culminating moment in a long and difficult process. Some carry the secret—and not-so-secret—knowledge of the falsifica-

---

* These statements as well as those concerning interviews are based upon my observations in both Santo Domingo and Santiago. The Consul General extended great courtesy by allowing me to observe almost all facets of the visa issuance process that took place in these offices. Since the time of this research the consulate in Santiago has been closed.

tions woven into their applications; one may have altered his birth certificate as to his age or parentage; another may be carrying a set of completely forged papers, arranged at a handsome fee; yet another may be assuming that the sum he paid someone who claimed friendship with the U.S. Consul will result in easy acquisition of the coveted consular stamp.

The hushed congregation at the U.S. Consulate and the tense groups nearby are in sharp contrast to the milling throngs outside the buildings of the national lottery, two blocks away. Here, a carnival atmosphere prevails. The crowds waiting to redeem winning tickets or hear the announcement of weekly drawings are generally poorly dressed, talking loudly among themselves with no apparent attempt on anyone's part to regulate them. Street vendors of food and clothing, and the ubiquitous *billeteros* (lottery ticket vendors) mingle freely with the crowd. Despite these superficial differences, the groups have much in common. Obtaining a U.S. visa and winning the lottery are both the culmination of a hopeful effort, aided by good luck, and the propitiation of whatever controlling forces there may be, human or superhuman.

RESIDENCE VISAS

Those at the consulate who are seeking approval for an immigrant visa request have usually completed numerous forms, many in English, secured various affidavits from local authorities, undergone a medical examination, and, above all, waited. Their waiting time may have been as short as three months or as long as five years, depending not only upon the procedural processes necessitated by the grounds of the application, but the time needed for any necessary review. In recent years, successful applicants have also had to wait for a quota number from the Western Hemisphere pool.

The interview concerning visa approval to which the applicant is summoned is probably his one face-to-face meeting with immigration officialdom. The applicant sits across from the visa officer, an American consular official, separated not only physically by the expanse of the desk, but by profound social and psychological factors. The examiner must render many judgments based upon sets of legal and cultural assumptions that may be at complete variance with those of the petitioners. Even though the printed Immigration and Nationality Act is 175 pages long, and the administrative and court decisions concerning immigration matters occupy volumes, the individual examiner is still faced with countless on-the-spot decisions. Actions which are interpreted by the applicants as unreasonable or unfair may be the product of a combination of the examiner's experience, knowledge of the intricacies of the law, and the pressures of the moment.

Basic changes in the law since 1968 make former routes of entrance into the United States, both procedural and physical, far more difficult for all Western Hemisphere residents. For example, formerly an applicant who could prove dependent status to any person legally residing in the United States could get a visa without much trouble. As many as qualified under this provision could enter. Since 1968 the sponsor of a spouse, minor child, or parent must have citizenship status in the United States in order to avoid waiting for an available quota number. Such distinctions and changes are seldom understood by the applicant, whose information about the procedures often comes from the previous experience of a family member or friend; this adds to the confusion surrounding the process of securing a visa. To the applicant, distinctions between residency and citizenship often appear arbitrary and unfair, because they are based upon cultural categories which do not coincide in the Dominican Republic and the United States.

An often heard complaint among Dominicans is that the U.S. government is prejudiced against illegitimate children. The law states that dependent children are eligible to be sponsored by their parents, and then devotes one full page to specifying the definition of such a child. However, it excludes certain categories which are socially legitimate according to Dominican norms. Thus, a child born in a polygamous relationship may be excluded from the U.S. even though he and his father, as well as their social peers, recognize a father-child relationship, with all the attendant obligations and sentiments.

Another example of such definitional conflict arises over norms that are applied to accepted marital arrangements. Arranged (*para negocio*) marriages are a common means of obtaining a residence visa. An individual legally residing in the United States agrees to marry a potential immigrant for a fee, usually at least $500, in return for using his position to "ask" for his spouse. The INS is acutely aware of this practice and attempts to prevent issuing visas in such cases. Thus, marital arrangements which seem unusual by middle-class American definition are open to serious question. It is not unusual, however, for girls of fifteen and sixteen to be married to older men in the Dominican Republic. In fact, it is valued, since the girl's extreme youth assures the man his wife is a virgin.

Lydia, 16, a resident of New York, was married on a visit to Aldea to her 24-year-old first cousin Tomás, who wished to migrate to join her. The marriage was one in which each expressed great affection for the other, demonstrated by weekly letters that passed between them. The marriage met widespread family approval, both because Tomás was known by everyone as a "serious" person, and because such a liaison cemented family relationships that could otherwise have led to potential conflict over inheritance rights. The wife held a job as a sewing machine operator, and arrangements were made for the couple to rent an apartment in the same building as her parents in upper Manhattan. After nearly a year of waiting, the application was rejected on the basis that Lydia was too young to be legally responsible for her husband's entrance. *

The different role perceptions of the consular officials was illustrated when two examiners, one male and the other female, discussed their job. The male took the position that once an individual seemingly met the criteria of the immigration law, it was the examiner's job to aid the applicant in obtaining a residence visa. The female, on the other hand, took the position that she was the last line of defense in making sure that those arriving in the U.S. were "fit to be there." Thus, she held up a visa on technical grounds because she personally disapproved a 26-year-old male married to a 50-year-old Puerto Rican female. She felt that even if the marriage had not been arranged purely to meet the legal requirements for immigration, then such a relationship was to be frowned upon because of the age difference between the spouses. Such inconsistencies of judgment do not go unnoticed by the applicants.

EMPLOYMENT PROSPECTS

An applicant with specific employment potential can obtain an immigrant visa on that basis. This potential may be the possession of advanced skill or technical knowledge that is in short supply in the United States. It may also be more particular, involving a temporary shortage in the United States, or a statement by an employer that he is unable to recruit employees domestically to perform certain tasks in a given location.

Those eligible to enter as workers in perennially understaffed fields are usually only those who have considerable education or training; relatively few Dominicans, especially *campesinos* from such places as Aldea, have had the opportunity to acquire this background. However, the Department of Labor periodically certifies a list of occupations in which workers are in temporarily short supply, as well as listing occupations in which workers are specifically not needed. Thus, a chef is allowed to enter, a cook's helper is not. Master tailors are given occupation-based visas; sewing machine operators are not. All persons

---

* This was one of a number of instances when my friendship with both parties, the husband while in Aldea and with his spouse in New York, brought forth expressions of deep distrust of my role as a researcher. The bride's parents were certain that I had been spying on her and that I was responsible for the refusal. The groom's brothers in New York approached me with thinly veiled threats if I did not come to Tomás' aid.

possessing a Ph.D. or those trained as chemists or accountants may enter without a prior job offer. This encourages applicants to exaggerate their skills if not to falsify them completely. Since the desired occupations list is updated from time to time, the potential immigrant is in effect forced to apply through knowledgeable visa brokers who can gain the most leverage according to the latest list. .

The most common employment factor in getting a visa is the statement by an employer that he needs aliens—or a particular alien—for a job because he can find no one in the United States to do that job. After the U.S. Labor Department receives this statement, it renders its judgment to the Immigration and Naturalization Service as to whether an employee is needed for the job in question. The process of finding individual employers willing to extend job offers to aliens by certifying that they can find no one in the domestic labor market to perform a needed task leads to a variety of arrangements, most of them involving third parties. Advertisements appear daily in Santo Domingo newspapers offering to help people find employers in the United States. In some cases family members already in New York make arrangements through their own personal knowledge of employers willing to sign such statements, or through brokers in New York. A number of individuals reported coming first to New York on a nonimmigrant visitors' visa, getting a job illegally, learning a skill, and then returning to Santo Domingo to apply for a residence visa based upon the former employer's willingness to make a formal request for them. Live-in maids are often brought in through this specific request category, and many Dominican females arrive under such auspices.

NONIMMIGRANT VISAS

The issuance of nonimmigrant visas is considered by most U.S. consulates to be quite routine. However, in the Dominican Republic it takes on a much different aspect. The sheer number of applicants coming to the small office presents management problems, and experience with a vast number of individuals who have violated their status means that each case demands an on-the-spot decision regarding the applicant's intent and probable future actions. The American Consul in Santo Domingo estimates that more than 35,000 Dominicans admitted as tourists live in the United States, working illegally (*El Caribe*, February 11, 1969); this figure may be grossly underestimated. Consequently, the local rule is that the applicant must present evidence that he has some reason to return to the Dominican Republic— some tangible resource such as owned property, a job with an income of over $150 per month, a bank account of long standing with sufficient funds to defray expenses of the vacation. Such "evidence" is, within the value system of the American officials, sufficient grounds for an individual to want to return. They are not unaware that there are ways to comply *pro forma* with these conditions, but, in reality, to circumvent them. What they seem less aware of is the different values placed upon them within the context of each party's culture. For one thing it is fairly easy to arrange for an employer, even a nonexistent employer, to write a letter indicating compliance with whatever conditions the consulate wishes to impose. An employee earning $140 per month is said to earn $180, a fictitious company complete with letterhead writes that an individual is employed by them, titles to property can be transferred temporarily into the aspirant's name, bank accounts opened with borrowed money.

Interviews for tourist visas are usually brief, lasting from three to fifteen minutes, depending upon how much perusal of the documents presented is necessary. A couple of perfunctory questions concerning the purpose and time of the trip, together with any necessary clarification of the documents presented, represents the typical interview. Upon this information the individual officer must make a decision. Approximately 50 percent of the applications are rejected. However, most of these are granted visas after a second or third attempt, once uncertainties are clarified. Many "unqualified" individuals apply repeatedly, to the annoyance of interviewing officers. One remarked, "Why must they come back and bother us?" after rejecting an individual who twice failed to supply documents indicating sufficient income. The following cases represent some of the requests handled by one visa officer during the course of a morning.

M.S., 56, married carpenter. Wants to visit friends in New York and Miami. Employed for a long period by an American living in Santiago and presents a letter of recommendation from him. A letter from a bank stated he had an account of over $500. At first the officer commented, "With a family, and long employment record it's not normal for a man his age to want to change his life pattern." However, in glancing through the bank letter a second time, he noted that the wording said that the individual had requested the letter for his "migration." Officer denied the visa and returned the letter without clarifying his objection. He told M.S. to ask bank to rewrite the letter and for him to return with the "corrected" copy.

O.B., 35, married mechanic with four children. Appeared for interview wearing oil-stained kahki uniform. Desired visa to go to San Juan to obtain parts for his auto repair shop. Has made two previous trips to Puerto Rico as a member of a sports team without incident. Documents indicated owner-ship of home, legal marriage, and children. Visa granted.

S.V., female, 40. Wants to visit her sick sister in New York for one week. Husband is dead. She claims ownership of a small grocery store (*pulpería*). Presented bank book indicating an account was opened two months previ-ously and now contains $350. Did not have house documents with her be-cause they were tied up in inheritance claim. In an aside in English the officer remarked to me, "It's difficult for me to believe she would spend all that money for one week." The visa was denied.

J.K., 19, student in local *colegio*. Desired to go to San Juan for a ten-day holiday. Father is physician. After the officer consulted with a young female secretary who knew the boy's family through an older sister, the visa was granted.

Almost every applicant, regardless of social and political rank, seems to undergo such waiting and scrutiny. Consular officers are particularly sensitive to charges of special privilege and bribery, and admit to exceptions only for individuals of political importance to the United States government. "Think how degrading it must be for a doctor to have to wait outside like that," commented one officer. However, the granting of multiple entry visas is common and even the most hum-ble individual is able to secure such a visa after a history of re-turning within the time limitation imposed by initial single entrance visa.

The popular conception of the difficulty of securing a visa of any kind was graphically illustrated by a cartoon appearing in *Cachafú* (June 9, 1969), a Dominican political satire magazine. It portrays a large, muscular woman, identified as the then-U.S. Vice-Consul in Santo Domingo, appearing at her office door with a large club in her hand, saying, "Let's have another applicant now." At her feet lies a figure with a bump on his head, surrounded by stars. On his buttocks is stamped "No visado" (visa refused). He is asking, "When is Nixon going to get that wild one out of here?"

ILLEGAL RESIDENCE

The term "illegal immigrant" conjures a vision of an individual wading across an unguarded river boundary in the dark of night, or jumping ship and swimming ashore. However, such a picture is far from accurate, especially among the New York immigrant groups. Many violate their status after arriving under quite public circum-stances. They most often come as tourists with valid nonimmigrant visas, and simply fail to leave when their visas expire. INS officials

were reluctant to discuss this issue as it in some cases involves U.S. domestic and foreign policy considerations.

A great many applicants for nonimmigrant visas state that their intention is to go to San Juan, Puerto Rico, for short vacations or to buy goods which are either unobtainable or more expensive in the Dominican Republic. Seventy-four percent of all temporary visitors from the Dominican Republic to the U.S. entered through San Juan in 1971 (INS 1971:65). For many San Juan is only a way station en route to New York. Opportunity for employment is better in San Juan than in Santo Domingo, but not nearly so remunerative as in New York. Once migrants have passed through the relatively easy INS inspection point at the San Juan airport, no further check of their documents is required, even if they go on to New York. It is fairly simple for Dominicans to identify themselves to English-speaking North American officialdom as Puerto Ricans.

Given the growing commercial and cultural interchange between Puerto Rico and the Dominican Republic, American consular officials are placed in an extremely difficult position in making decisions regarding nonimmigrant visas. There is always the possibility of offending someone by rejecting legitimate requests, and officers are keenly aware of criticism they think unjustified when a "flap" develops because of a wrong decision. At the same time, they feel their close scrutiny justified when what seems to be a valid request turns out to be merely a ruse to circumvent legal entry into the United States.*

It is not really known, at least publicly, how many of those granted visitors' visas violate their status by remaining to work. Official records only indicate the number of persons required to depart after being formally charged by INS. Far more common, but unreported, are occasions when individuals are contacted by INS agents and allowed to depart from the United States without official action being taken. The individual can then reapply for a visa without a record of previous violation of visa status.

* Two examples are cited as justification for such close scrutiny and even cynicism about the motives of applicants for tourists' visas. In 1968 the American Consul was requested by an official of a Dominican trade union organization to grant temporary visas for a delegation of Dominican unionists to meet with their Puerto Rican counterparts in San Juan. After arriving in San Juan and clearing U.S. customs agents, this group headed directly for a previously arranged chartered plane and flew on to New York. Months later only half the group had been located by INS authorities and returned to Santo Domingo. During Christmas vacation of 1968 a priest in Santo Domingo requested and was granted visas for his choir to give a concert in Puerto Rico. Since he had personally made the request of the American Consul General for the group's visas, he felt responsible concerning his own credibility to the Americans. Consequently, when they arrived in San Juan, he collected all passports and kept them until the return flight. Still, two members of the choir chose to remain illegally and did not return with the group.

TABLE 6. ALIENS REQUIRED TO DEPART

Nationality	1968	1969	1970	1971
Mexico	21,227	23,837	20,854	21,779
Canada	3,439	3,562	3,671	3,213
Jamaica	2,517	1,926	1,460	1,838
United Kingdom	2,015	1,827	1,851	1,727
Dominican Republic	1,721	1,655	1,679	2,536
Philippines	1,658	1,853	1,968	1,524
Trinidad	1,721	1,192	1,123	1,269
Italy	997	1,122	1,072	1,142
Guatemala	979	941	1,504	1,321
Greece	943	1,116	1,107	1,161
Ecuador	860	1,195	1,116	1,302
Columbia	808	1,307	1,625	2,014

Source: INS Annual Reports

ILLEGAL ENTRY

So far we have discussed only legal and semilegal acts of entry into the United States by Dominican citizens. It is also possible to obtain completely falsified visas for prices ranging to $1,000 or even higher. The extent of this completely illegal activity is only hinted at in official statements. Its existence is more often brought to light in newspaper accounts of arrests, and occasional public comment by consular officials. In early 1969 the activity was brought to public attention by the arrest of a band of visa falsifiers who had in their possession at the time of arrest 40 Dominican passports bearing the imprint of a U.S. visa stamp.

[Two individuals] were integral members of a band of criminals who operated on a national scale, swindling lower class people principally *campesinos* from the interior of the country . . . [including the Aldea area]. They said that [the head] operated an *agencia tributaria* [in Santo Domingo]. Both were involved in attempting to help obtain supposed U.S. visas in the American Consulate for sums varying from $RD400-500. The passports were returned to their owners with false visas. They utilized the signature of [the] Vice Consul . . . who discharges this function in the consulate. Using materials and machines of the same type that are used by the consular officials, they made a falsification considered by the police to be almost perfect (*Listín-Diario*, February 13, 1969).

As an aftermath of the exposé that took place after this arrest, the American Consul General in Santo Domingo publicly petitioned the President of the Republic at a consulate press conference, asking the Dominican government to try harder to stem the illegalities involved in procuring U.S. visas, noting that very often the falsified documents originate in the government offices themselves.

The [U.S. Consul] showed "surprise" at what he considered alarming cases of falsified documents that are being presented to obtain U.S. visas. [The Consul] explained that there are those who falsify property titles, birth certificates, bank books and other documents that are necessary in order to be granted residence and tourist visas (*El Caribe*, February 11, 1969).

The Dominican government's attitude toward the problem was expressed by the President's rebuttal several days later at his own press conference. "The government does everything possible to stop the commission of fraud in the publication of official documents. . . . Nevertheless, . . . fraud exists here and everywhere else in the world" (*El Caribe*, February 14, 1969).

The charge is constantly made, and believed by most Dominicans, that consular officials are implicated in this illegal activity, and that for a price and with the proper connections, anyone can get a visa. As indicated by the President's statement, this kind of activity is accepted, if not expected, within the Dominican socioeconomic context. Thus, when individuals claim special friendships that will help applicants get visas, they are believed. The leader of the falsification ring mentioned earlier made just such a claim to prospective clients in his role as *tributario;* the Consul contended that an American could not have been implicated since the clue to which visas were falsified was in the misspelling of the word application with only one p, making it similar to Spanish *aplicación.*

Gonzales remarks:

It is interesting to note, though, that the Dominicans base their expectations not only on the personalistic and paternalistic patterns taught them by their own culture, but upon observation of actual consular activity itself. Since ultimately, the Consul himself has to make a judgment on each individual, and since he frequently has too little information upon which to base this judgment, he may very well be swayed by having a recommendation from a mutual friend. This quite natural circumstance may be carried even further, however, when a trusted friend approaches the Consul and asks him directly to give a visa to a friend, relative, *compadre,* or worker. Although the U.S. Consular Service dislikes admitting it, it is clear that patronage operates in the American socio-cultural system as well. When one considers the total number of visa applications, it is true that those granted to favored individuals are a small fraction, but it takes only a few such cases for the rumor to spread and the belief to take root.

. . . although many Dominicans are able to obtain favors from the U.S. Consulate, they are not generally of the social class which finds it necessary to sell the visas for money. They value their contacts more for the power and prestige it gives them than for the financial return [1971:164].

Illegal entry may also involve indirect routes through neighboring countries, but this is rare because of the time and expense involved. No informant in New York claimed to have used such routings, although some could discuss them with detail. For example, by going first to Curacao, from there to the U.S. Virgin Islands, and thence to San Juan or even directly on to New York, it is possible to take advantage of special diplomatic and trading relations in existence in the Caribbean which allow relatively uninhibited inter-island passage.

In October 1969, press reports told of a group of 70 Dominicans stranded in Baranquilla, Colombia.

According to them they came to Colombia in an excursion group organized by their fellow countrymen Thelma Sanchez and Juan Mendez who offered to secure U.S. visas there so that they could get work in the U.S.

Nevertheless since the 13th of August when they arrived here, the Dominicans have not been able to obtain the documents. The U.S. Consulate notified them they can only secure them in their own country.

On the other hand, according to the members of the group, the organizers of the excursion had neither communicated with them nor given any aid since they arrived (*El Caribe*, October 27, 1969).

Several weeks later the Dominican government sent a plane to Colombia to return this band of its citizens home.

At about the same time, five Dominicans were deported from Miami after spending four months in jail.

According to them they came to the capital (Santo Domingo) from their village looking for a U.S. visa. They said a fellow who they identified only by the name of Guzman offered to get visas for them for RD$200 per person. A few days after receiving his money he gave them their passports which had been provided with apparently valid visas. Guzman accompanied them to Miami and everyone entered without any problem.

Once in Miami Guzman stated that they could go to any place in the U.S. they wanted to go to seek work. He left the group, taking their passports with him. Guzman, they said, flew on to New York. They boarded a bus for New York but in Jacksonville the authorities required their travel documents and they were detained (*El Caribe*, October 21, 1969).

Social Implications of Visa Requirements and Procedures

For the vast majority of Dominicans, and particularly for migrants from Aldea, the requirements and administration of U.S. immigration law serves to reinforce certain traditional relationships, and to reinterpret others. The very process of immigrating entails negotiating the labyrinth of immigration law and the bureaucratic procedures that implement it, which place great emphasis on certain types of kin and broker relationships. By placing the individual in a relationship of obligation to a sponsor already in the U.S., and limiting sponsorship to certain categories of kin, the law functions to reinforce the existing values of familial ties, especially those of the nuclear family.

Those unable to obtain visas based upon kinship, who instead find employer-sponsors, arrive in New York not only to already existing social networks, but laden with social and economic obligations. The employer arrangements are usually made by kin already in New York, often in conjunction with professional brokers. The obligations incurred when an individual's visa is the direct result of someone else's intercession are many, and not easily discharged. In addition, dependent social relationships result from the tenuous legal positions of many immigrants; the threat of denunciation of illegal entrants or residents is inherent in any break in friendly relations.

The administration of U.S. immigration law, with its bureaucratic maze of paperwork, restrictions, and delays, is part of a familiar phenomenon in the Republic, and does not surprise most Dominicans. But many Dominicans also perceive the law as just another aspect of the political and economic imperialism that has manifested itself in the historical relationship between the two countries, and consequently, is to be at least ignored and at most violated whenever possible. Thus, the law reinforces many negative attitudes toward the United States, attitudes which remain barely hidden among large segments of the immigrant group.

Although the consular officers frequently feel that the people are trying to lie and cheat their way into the United States, the fact is that most people simply want to go, and they cannot really understand why they should not be permitted to do so. Their interpretation is that the United States consular agency is required to do everything it can to make it difficult for them, but they see this as being a challenge. Since legal and governmental procedures in their own country are frequently tangled in red tape, they do not criticize the United States for this—they are accustomed to it. Cleverness in outwitting "the system" pays off in visas granted as well as in higher prestige (Gonzales 1970:163).

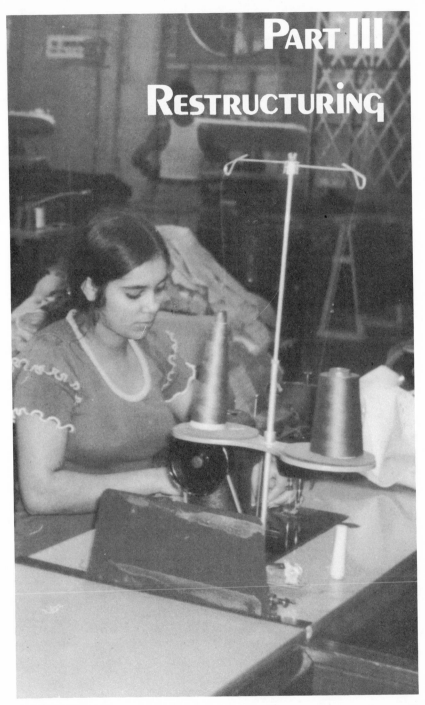

PART III
RESTRUCTURING

FROM DREAM TO REALITY: *The garment industry provides work for many Dominicans once they reach New York.*

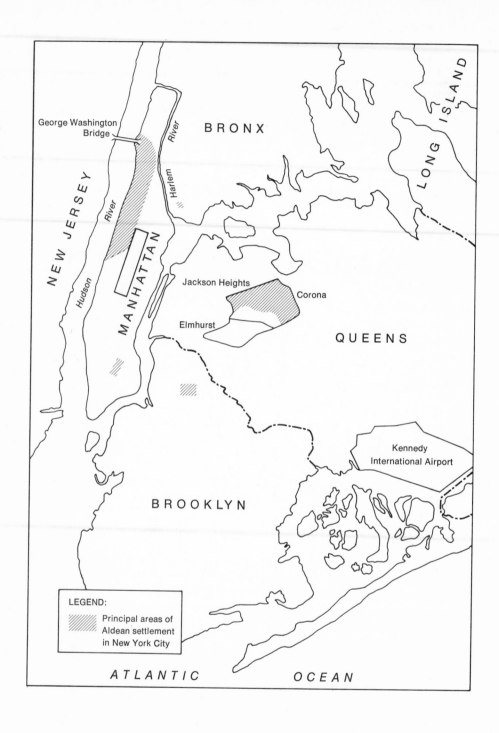

George Washington
Bridge

BRONX

NEW JERSEY

Hudson River

Harlem River

MANHATTAN

Jackson Heights

Elmhurst

Corona

QUEENS

LONG ISLAND

Kennedy
International Airport

BROOKLYN

LEGEND:

Principal areas of
Aldean settlement
in New York City

ATLANTIC   OCEAN

CHAPTER FIVE

The New York Experience

We have so far examined a number of facets of life in the Dominican Republic which demonstrate that as a result of migration and culture contact with North Americans, both presocialization for migration and a reordering of elements in the social structure at both the national and village level have taken place. We now shift our attention and perspective to New York. While physically far removed from their native island, Aldeanos in New York are participants in a field of social relations encompassing both places. In this chapter and those that follow, special attention is given to the examination of the processes by which individuals and groups seek accommodation to their new social environment.

Entry

It must be remembered that at this point in the history of the Dominican migration to New York, the immigrant seldom arrives as a social isolate, unknown and unknowing, forced to cope with his new environment alone. The very nature of the process of recruitment into the United States almost obliges the individual to have some pre-existing social linkages to New York. This may be due to visa law requirements, the obligations involved in accumulating passage and bonding money, or simply the result of the vast number of his countrymen already present. Indeed, it was difficult to elicit responses to a hypothetical question about the actions of someone arriving without knowing anybody. They simply could not imagine such a situation. "If you don't have family, at least you would have the address of friends of friends. When I said that I was going to New York, a lot of people just gave me the name of their brother or friend here to see. I came with a whole list of names," said a single, female, illegal immigrant, with only fictive members of her kin network living in the city. Even doña Eva, credited by the villagers as being the first to travel to New York in the late 1940's, was recruited through an older relative who had found his way to the United States much earlier.

The new arrival is most likely to be met at Kennedy Airport by someone already known to him, usually his sponsor in the immigration process. The arrival gate of planes from Santo Domingo is normally chaotic, as large groups wait to greet relatives or old friends. On occasion individuals arrive without these reception contingents to greet them, but in such cases they most often have either met someone on the flight with whom some arrangement for transportation to the city has been made, or they recognize someone who has come to greet another person, and on-the-spot arrangments can be made. Thus, in few cases does an individual arrive alone; almost immediately he begins to participate in a pre-existing social network in which the majority of the participants are already known to him in varying degrees and serve to guide him through the initial confrontation with his new physical and social environment.

Initially, accommodations are arranged for by the sponsor, usually within his own household. If there is no room in the sponsor's household, another place is found. The expectation, especially if the recruit is an unattached kinsman, is that he will live in the household as a contributing member. Certainly it would be unthinkable for the immigrant to be sent to any commercial establishment during this initial period, or even that at any time a single person should live apart by himself. Some households are particularly responsive to taking in temporary occupants.* These are not necessarily dormitories, but are usually households most of whose members consider their presence in New York quite temporary and especially welcome additional contributions to rent payment and food expenses. Crowding is common; privacy is seldom experienced in the village, and so is not missed in the city. There is some grumbling about personal things being used without permission, but on the whole there is remarkably little interpersonal friction.

The relationship between the sponsor and the recruit usually involves more than sentiments of kinship and friendship. Legal as well as financial relations may be involved. The New York resident may act as a bondsman, assuring the INS the recruit will not be a financial burden to the United States government, or pay for the passage to the

---

* The term "roomers" commonly used in this context would indicate a separate room for the individual. This is seldom the case as such isolation is considered neither necessary nor desirable. Quite commonly at nighttime every room in a household has one or more sleeping occupants.

United States. Willingness to place oneself in the role of sponsor can stem from several sources: heavy social obligation toward those within his affective network of kin and acquaintances; the prospect of release from the actual or potential obligation of sending remittances to Aldea —the new recruit can be expected to share in turn the burden of providing for those remaining in the village. More indirect reasons for sponsorship include the public recognition of his identity as a *persona de confianza*. For some, sponsoring kinsmen has economic advantage: they contribute toward specific economic goals, helping with rent or house payments, or participating in small business enterprises. One individual, reputed to be the wealthiest of all the New York residents from Aldea, has been able to amass considerable economic and social power by underwriting, owning, or operating a collection of small businesses run by immigrants he is credited with having sponsored to New York.

Soon after he arrives, the immigrant is taken by his sponsor to greet mutual acquaintances and kinsmen. Often he carries written or verbal messages as well as small presents from individuals in Aldea. This initial visiting pattern provides an opportunity to exchange information and gossip about the village and other New York residents. If no job has been previously arranged, this visiting pattern includes a search for possible employment situations which may be known among the individuals visited. Thus, for the newly arrived, as well as for many other individuals, two basic problems demand attention: finding suitable employment, and seeking out living accommodations which they can afford and at the same time will not isolate them from friends and kinsmen.

Employment

The search for a job begins almost immediately. Very often the recruit arrives to find a position awaiting him, procured by his sponsor at his own place of work or scouted out for him among the sponsor's network of acquaintances. But the list of jobs for which he is qualified is severely circumscribed—he is usually totally unskilled. If he is recruited directly out of the village he is minimally acquainted with machinery, let alone factory systems of production. In addition, his inability to communicate in English makes him suited only to jobs where such communication is unessential or where others can serve as translators. The single most common entry level job indicated by informants was washing dishes in restaurants. The clothing industry also attracts many since it had prior to the Dominican influx adapted itself to Puerto Rican employees and worked out organizational patterns including bilingual supervisors or mediators between management and employees.

Two cousins, one from Aldea and the other from a village 40 kilometers away, own a small loft factory on the Lower East Side. The nonunionized factory does subcontract piece-work for a larger clothing manufacturer. The 27 employees are all Dominicans from the two villages and can trace relationships, both real and fictive, of kinship with one another. An English-speaking Cuban is a part-time bookkeeper and is the only outsider involved in the operation. Lunch is purchased by most of the employees from a nearby restaurant owned by an Aldeano.

TABLE 7. OCCUPATIONS HELD BY IMMIGRANTS FROM ALDEA

	Male	Female	Total
Barbers and beauticians	4	1	5
Building superintendents	5		5
Elevator operators	6		6
Entrepreneurs			
Clothing manufacturers	3		3
Grocery stores (bodegas)	7		7
Hardware (partners)	3		3
Travel agency	1		1
Factory, garments			
Operators, cutters, pressmen	49	43	92
Factory, general			
Laborers	40	6	46
Machine operators	18	6	24
Assemblers	4	7	11
Household workers		2	2
Office clerks		3	3
Porters, janitors, custodians	11		11
Restaurant workers			
Busboys	11		11
Cooks, ass't cooks	4		4
Countermen	3		3
Dishwashers, cleaners	43		43
Waiters	1		1
Skilled and semi-skilled workers			
Auto-body repairmen	3		3
Mechanics	4		4
Painters	1		1
Plumbers and steam fitters	2		2
Stevedores	5		5
Store clerks	2	9	11
Taxi drivers	2		2

None of the so-called skilled individuals is a recognized member of a craft; they have learned their trade in on-the-job situations and are employed by small nonunionized firms.

Sergio secured a job in a small auto repair shop as a helper and cleaner shortly after his arrival. He began helping primarily in the body repair section and after three years was skilled enough to get a job in another small shop as their body man. His salary is about 80 percent of what he would get in a union shop. However, the informality of the job situation allows considerable additional income through overtime and performing some work privately at home using tools borrowed for the weekend. This home repair service is confined largely to work for his network of Dominican friends. Seldom is this work done on an exchange of cash basis but rather an exchange of work and mutual assistance obligations.

Many other workers are members of unskilled trade unions in such areas as garment-making or the restaurant trade. The marginality and vulnerability of many of these workers in relation to union activity can be illustrated in two ways. On a number of occasions when informants were discussing salaries with me, payroll slips were brought forth. The union dues check-off item was referred to as the "union tax." The union was perceived as but another "obligation," and my informants had only the vaguest understanding of their relation to it. In turn, unions seldom knew or were willing to discuss their membership in ethnic terms. Few Spanish-speaking individuals are officers in unions such as the ILGWU, even though a large percentage of its members are Hispanos. Immigrant workers contemplating unionization are vulnerable to management threats. According to stories corroborated by the union involved, a large restaurant chain was able to intimidate a group of Hispano kitchen workers who were attempting to organize by threatening to give their names to the Immigration and Naturalization Service and have them sent back to their home countries. This can be done only when the individual is working illegally, but such statements are readily believed, and an individual whose position in the social and economic system is marginal—even if his presence in the U.S. is legal—is easily cowed.

A significant part of the individual's employment strategy is linked to the ties he retains to the Republic and the nature of their claims on him. Annual journeys back to the village for extended periods of time require a job that allows for such mobility. One of the reasons that the clothing industry appeals to large numbers of Dominicans is the extended lay-offs that occur during seasonal changeovers, particularly in summer, allowing for visits home without the risk of losing one's job. At the same time, the decentralized nature of the industry, with numerous small factories, makes for worker mobility, so that if an immigrant wishes to return to the Republic for the winter months, he can assume that a similar job will be available in another factory when he returns. Restaurant helpers are equally mobile. The penalty for acquiring a more stable job is the commitment to New York rather than Aldea which such a job implies.

Favio and Rudolpho were cousins who came to New York at the same time and soon secured work as kitchen helpers in a small Hungarian restaurant. After about a year the owner-chef told both he would teach them to cook and they became his assistants. However, when both decided they wanted to go visit their families in Aldea, the owners gave them the option of leaving and returning as dishwashers or remaining until the restaurant closed for its annual vacation and retaining their cooks' jobs. Favio decided on the latter course and arranged for the migration of his wife and small child to New York, while Rudolpho chose the former and returned to the village for two months and came back to his less remunerative job. "Someone to scrub pots can always be found, while cooks we have to depend upon," commented the owner.

In the decade since the Dominican immigration to New York began, employment has generally been readily obtainable, even for the unskilled. In discussing the job market, most informants insisted that with enough persistence some work could always be found; the problem was not merely finding a job, but finding a "good" job. They often made unfavorable comparisons between Dominicans, whom "the boss recognizes as hard workers," and Puerto Ricans and blacks, portrayed by Dominicans as lazy and willing to live on welfare. Even if such a comparison is valid, it fails to recognize that by and large, most Dominicans in New York are physically and socially able to participate in the labor force. The immigration process filters out those who are incapacitated, or too old, or too young to be readily employable. Since the possession of immigrant visa status is essential to participation in any form of public welfare assistance, all individuals present illegally are automatically precluded from seeking such help.

The social organization indigenous to this group, as well as the variant forms which emerge to cope with the New York situation, serve to make the individual employable or to lessen the burden of unemployment. A mother who wishes or needs to work usually has access to an extended family system which will as a matter of course assume responsibility for her children, either in the village or in New York. Elderly parents may be brought to New York for the express purpose of caring for children, or the children may be sent back to live with them. In the summer of 1970, a period of economic recession, many clothing factories closed down for extended layoffs. One option for many Aldeanos employed in these factories was to return to the Republic temporarily; especially for older people, two or three months in the village is cheaper than a comparable time in New York. In both Aldea and New York, the unemployed individual is normally a participant in an extended network whose members are morally bound to sustain him during this period. It is hard to tell how long this mutual aid system would last during a period of prolonged unemployment; this has not been put to the test since the Dominican migration became widespread.

There is, as yet, no evidence of any marked effect on Dominican immigration patterns due to changes in economic conditions and consequent availability of employment in the U.S.* Any variations in the influx of these migrants is related to domestic political events in both countries, such as the Revolution of 1965 and the change in U.S. immigration law. Undoubtedly any improvement in the economic situation in the Republic would only increase the pressures for out-migration as more individuals achieved the necessary resources to leave.

Housing and Settlement Patterns

Finding adequate housing is a problem for all New Yorkers; it is compounded for some by limited resources and racial and cultural discrimination. Despite the stereotype that Spanish-speaking people live only in *barrios* such as Spanish Harlem, Hispanos are widely distributed throughout the city.** The misconception that all Hispanos are *barrio* residents is in part a result of the difficulty many people have in distinguishing between Puerto Ricans and other Spanish-speaking segments of the population. Since statistics used in the 1960's were based on 1960 census figures—preceding the great influx of non-Puerto Rican Hispanos—all dark-skinned residents speaking Spanish are classified as Puerto Ricans.*** Thus, large blocks of Hispanos are

---

* See Alvarez, *Return Migration to Puerto Rico,* for a discussion of the impact of U.S. economic and demographic conditions upon the pattern of Puerto Rican migration to and from the mainland United States.

** I have been the guest in the Fifth Avenue apartments of one Dominican and several wealthy Cubans. These individuals were very conscious of their own Hispanic cultural background and extremely nationalistic. Nevertheless, their economic resources, education, and sophistication allowed them to participate selectively in a variety of cultural milieus, and they were barely cognizant of the life style of the group on which this study focuses.

*** In Queens, especially in the Jackson Heights and Corona area, there are large numbers of South Americans, Dominicans, and Cubans, but relatively few Puerto Ricans. The community relations specialist in the office of the Queens District Attorney, basing his information on the 1960 census, rightfully claimed there were few Puerto Ricans in Queens. This in turn was interpreted by the staff of this office to mean, "There is no Spanish Problem." Hence, no provisions were made for Spanish-speaking personnel in this office. The fact that few of these non-Puerto Ricans obtain U.S. citizenship, and are not voters, is undoubtedly important in this "official blindness."

ignored. In addition, the generally low socioeconomic level and accompanying lack of acculturation and participation in the dominant society contribute to the limited visibility of Dominican and other Hispanic residents in areas of the city where they are less concentrated than in the well-known *barrios*.

Dominicans in New York are concentrated in three areas—the Jackson Heights-Corona section of Queens, the Lower East Side of Manhattan in the heart of what was once an almost exclusively Italian enclave, and the Upper West Side of Manhattan from the 70's to the George Washington Bridge. In addition, more and more Dominicans are moving to Brooklyn and the Bronx. While the Dominican population is concentrated in three areas, it is not accurate to assume that they live only in these places, or that they have established communities to the exclusion of other ethnic groups from those neighborhoods.*

There is a rough hierarchy of living areas. Some of the first Aldeano immigrants found dwellings on the Lower East Side, close to the clothing manufacturing lofts where many had jobs. Rent still is

---

* The difficulty maintaining ethnic exclusiveness is apparent in the reaction of Italians in both Corona and in the Lower East Side to a perceived threat. In the latter area "Little Italy" is being encroached on from all sides; the expanding Chinese community directly south of it buys buildings previously inhabited exclusively by Italians; to the east and north Spanish-speaking groups now inhabit what once were the dwellings of Jews and Italians. In the window of the office of the Italian-American Civil Rights League in the heart of "Little Italy" is a sign admonishing Italians to "Keep Our Community Together, Register Vacant Apartments Here."

In an interesting contrast, during fifteen months of field work in New York I observed two Bronx buildings change from primarily Puerto Rican and black occupants to exclusively Dominicans. Most of these, from a village near Aldea, could trace some real or fictive kinship relationship to one another. Their actions illustrate how pockets of Dominicans are established. Octavio, his wife, unmarried daughter, and a *compadre* found a vacant apartment here and formed a household unit. When Octavio's two teen-age sons arrived the *compadre* took over a just vacated apartment in the building and rented rooms to other unattached males, all of whom were friends and acquaintances from the village. Meanwhile, Octavio became the superintendent of this and an adjoining building. The next vacancy was taken over by a married daughter who had been living on the Upper West Side in Manhattan. The wife of the *compadre* arrived, as did Octavio's five youngest children, who had been left temporarily in the village by their parents. Other apartments were rented to Dominicans as they became available. (The rapid evacuation by former tenants leads one to suspect flight.) At this point the entire eight units of one of the buildings were occupied by persons who were intimate acquaintances of one another. Whereas prior to this time the front door had been almost always propped open and the individual apartment doors locked, the reverse was now true. Children wandered from household to household, being both fed and corrected by any adult present. In the same manner the adults now moved about visiting and performing acts of mutual aid. Octavio, in discussing the move of his daughter and son-in-law, justified it by remarking, "They [his children and grandchildren] must come to know their family. It is better this way or we will grow apart." It is interesting and important to note that at any given point in time someone from this interconnected household, now numbering over 40 persons, could be found departing, visiting, or arriving from the Dominican Republic. Several times a month a telephone call was made from this extended household in New York to Santiago, for social and business purposes.

extremely cheap, although the buildings often are very old and ill-kept. Three-room apartments can be found here for as little as $35 a month. This area is considered by most to be the least desirable as it is the most crowded and without access to parks or other open spaces. Parents of small children complain especially of the "bad influence" of the neighborhood. It is here that open conflict periodically erupts between various national and ethnic groups. Just blocks away is the heart of the Bowery, notorious for its drunken derelicts. However, the neighborhood's low rents and proximity to work, and subway lines by which one can visit those living in other parts of the city, provide sufficient reason to remain.

In the early 1960's the first known Dominican from the Cibao moved to the Corona area of Queens. This transitional area next to Flushing Meadows had earlier been populated by Germans, Irish, and later Italians; after World War II blacks bought property in the area, and this group, composed largely of civil servants, in turn became part of the rush to the mushrooming suburbs on Long Island. They gladly sold or rented their aging two-story houses to Dominicans and other Latin Americans. The prices paid were often highly inflated—according to a local real estate agent, rents and sale prices could be doubled by such transactions, even though some of the long-time residents, especially the Italians, resisted the influx of this new group of "foreigners." Today probably upwards of 1500 residents of this portion of Corona alone come from the village of Aldea and neighboring regions of the Cibao. A thriving hardware store, four restaurants, two barber shops, three grocery stores, and a gift shop are owned by former residents of the village. In addition, a real estate firm, a travel agency, a jewelry store and a carpenter shop are owned by other Dominicans. Two small garment factories owned and staffed by Dominicans are to be found in this area.

The high prices for living accommodations can be paid only through a household organization of high density, in which most of the occupants contribute financially.

Ramon, 25, arrived in 1966, the first of his family to migrate. Within a year he was joined by a younger brother, and in late 1968 by his mother, father, and teen-aged brother and sister. Four younger siblings remain in Aldea, cared for by the father's brother who also cultivates the 15 *tareas* of land still held by the migrating family. Ramon pays $185 a month to rent a four-room flat in a building owned by a Venezuelan. In addition, a cousin and the son of a *compadre*, both still in their teens, reside in the apartment. The sleeping arrangements are such that four males sleep in one bedroom, the parents and their daughter in another, and the cousin, who works a night shift, sleeps alone in a tiny third bedroom. All are working at unskilled jobs in Long Island factories, earning $70 to $80 per week, *límpio*. The income of the nuclear family is pooled and the others pay room and board.

Estaban arrived in 1961, and after three years moved from Manhattan to Corona. A year later he bought a house there for $28,000. The three floors are occupied by kinsmen, together with a shifting population of single males from the village. Recently Estaban paid $40,000 for an adjoining house which has five living units. All are now filled with kinsmen or friends, most of whom were brought to New York through Estaban's arrangements for money and visas. Obviously he could only have accomplished these purchases through extensive borrowing arrangements with high monthly payments. However, his rental income is more than adequate to enable him to meet his loan obligations.

Adjacent to the Corona district in Queens are Jackson Heights and Elmhurst, both areas of better housing, with many large apartment houses built within the last two decades. Both areas have become the residential centers for lower-middle-class Latin Americans, including upwardly mobile Puerto Ricans. A few Aldeanos have moved into the area after first living elsewhere. This not only represents status improvement but also has the advantage of gaining better housing, often at the same or lower prices. However, high density apartment dwelling, i.e., crowded conditions due to many persons sharing a single unit, is apparently not accepted here. The proximity of Jackson Heights to Corona, Queens allows individuals to maintain regular intimate linkages to their older established social network.

Nefte, 37, and her husband Eduardo, 40, are both from large and proper families in the village. Through night school and his initial work in a restaurant, he learned enough English to be hired as a bilingual salesman in a large store in Queensboro Plaza. Nefte worked for the first few years in New York, but now is a full-time homemaker caring for their two children. She has sixteen brothers and sisters in New York; most of them live in Corona as do several of Eduardo's seven siblings. On weekends Nefte and Eduardo are frequently to be found visiting people in Corona, or even in Manhattan, especially when they accompany their parents during their now almost annual trips to New York. Rent for a three-bedroom apartment in Jackson Heights is only $25 a month more than that paid by a younger brother who lives with six small children in a crowded one-bedroom flat in Corona.

Another housing variation can be found on the Upper West Side and in the Bronx, where large apartments are available. Here one finds dormitory-type arrangements, with provisions either for boarding or for common cooking facilities. The renters are seldom related but often know one another from the Republic, or have been referred by mutual acquaintances. However, very few individuals from Aldea were found to occupy such units as the expectation is for them to live in a household made up of members of their preexisting network of family and acquaintances. The occupants of dormitories are much more likely to come from urban areas of Santo Domingo or Santiago.

Apparently very few Dominicans reside in public housing units, partly because of their recent arrival on the New York scene and the tremendously long waiting lists for this kind of housing.

José, a 35-year-old taxi driver, the son of doña Nina, came to New York in 1960. He and his wife lived in an apartment on the Upper West Side which was torn down in the urban renewal of that area. As a result, he now lives in a pleasant three-bedroom apartment in a public housing unit on an avenue near his old apartment. They like the space and the comfort of the apartment but are regretful that they have no family around; his wife has never learned English and feels especially isolated. He is concerned about the "American influence on his children" that comes from having no other family members nearby.

FURNISHINGS

Typically, household furnishings are spare and simple. They differ most markedly from those in a typical American home by their lack of textured textile surfaces. The warm, moist atmosphere of a tropical climate makes such materials undesirable, and only a few of the hundreds of Hispano-occupied apartments I entered during my New York field work had, for example, any floor covering other than linoleum. Similarly, most homes have sofas and overstuffed chairs, some expensive pieces of furiture, all covered with clear plastic fitted covers. This practice is so common that a whole industry has developed making plastic furniture covers and catering primarily to the Latin American population in the U.S.

In keeping with the austerity conveyed by linoleum and plastic, is the absence of room adornment such as ornamental pictures or knicknacks. Except for framed photographic portraits, formally inscribed diplomas, or, occasionally, portraits of the Madonna, the walls are barren. A bouquet of plastic flowers in a vase may well be the only room decoration. Aside from the plastic covered sofa and chairs, the other usual living room object is frequently an expensive television- and radio-phonograph unit.

This barrenness is not, as I at first assumed, a direct translation of the norm of household furnishing in the rural Dominican Republic, the result of the economic status of the household, or the adaptation of a household with many children. Rather, few individuals, even after long periods of time in the U.S., are committed and this style of furnishing reflects their lack of such commitment. The items purchased are either customary or functional in the Dominican Republic. Indeed, informants in discussing their home furnishings often made reference to its transportability as well as its usefulness "in my country."

Mario, 33, has lived in New York for eight years and is employed as a cleaner in Lincoln Center. He speaks functional English and, of all my close informants, he was probably the most acculturated. He had few ties to the Republic as he had no extended family there; his wife's entire family lives in New York. I had assumed he thought of himself as a fairly permanent New York resident, even though he did not "want to become an American." One day he, his wife, and I went shopping for a new set of bedroom furniture for their personal use. The criteria throughout the discussion was whether a given piece had features which made it feasible to use in Santo Domingo, *"cuando regresemos"* (when we return).

Typology of Commitment

Not unlike many immigrant populations, few individuals arrive from Santo Domingo with the idea of permanent settlement in New York. A great many, because they do not hold residence visas, cannot make such long-term plans in the first place. Regardless of their status, most arrive with the idea of remaining only long enough to accumulate through hard work and thrift enough capital to return home and buy land, build a house, or set themselves up in a small business. Even those from urban areas express this attitude toward their presence in New York. Within the village there are enough individuals who have successfully made the journey to New York and back to make it appear a viable possibility. Large parts of newly built urban residential developments in the Dominican Republic are being purchased by New York residents; they make monthly payments to Dominican land development speculators for future homes. Politically oriented members of the Dominican colony in New York work endlessly to build a political base upon which to return to power in Santo Domingo. They repeatedly remind others that the present president of the Republic, Balaguer, built a power base for his eventual return to the island while living in New York.

The manner in which the individual resolves the issue of his personal commitment to permanent settlement in New York is of great importance in understanding the strategies he selects for coping with life there. His willingness to learn English, patterns of housing and employment, use of leisure time, even the nature of his household furnishings depend upon how he perceives his situation at a given point in time. While individual life histories remain idiosyncratic in detail, it is possible to develop a typology of immigrant commitment to permanent residence in New York. Such a typology is based upon salient factors of: visa status; nature of linkages to the Republic, both social and economic; age and sex; length of time in the United States; and experiential factors.

In the graphic presentation of this typology the commitment to removal ranges from temporary to permanent. Thus, one is theoretically, and actually, able to locate individuals who are in New York for a one- or two-week visit as well as those with no intention of ever returning to the Dominican Republic. The vertical dimension orders social, temporal, and ecological factors. Obviously all these factors are interdependent: any one may be demonstrated to be a function of another. They are intended as a heuristic conceptualization (the observer's model) rather than clearly delineated categories as perceived by the social actor, the immigrant himself.

Visa status. As has been shown, the immigrant's visa status weighs heavily on the nature of individual's day-to-day as well as long-range activities. Especially for those present illegally, there is great pressure to maximize every opportunity to work and save.

Linkages to the Republic. Here we are referring to the presence or absence of important kin and friends (social linkages) as well as economic ties such as property ownership or inheritance prospects. Loosening of these ties need not break the linkages. More often, it indicates the other members of these social dyads have shifted residence to New York, or that the individual has acquired economic attachments in New York.

Age and sex. Generally speaking, the older the individual at the time of migration, the more likely it is that his sojourn will be relatively brief. However, females who have taken on new roles outside the household are less likely to express interest in returning.

Lenth of time in New York. As might be expected, the longer an individual resides outside the Republic, the more satisfied he tends to become with continued residence in New York. This is highly related to his linkage to the Republic, as over a period of time members of the individual's kin network have usually been recruited to New York. This time order reverses itself as retirement approaches. Then the almost universal expectation is that the individual will move back to the Republic, though annual trips to the United States may continue.

Experiential factors. This is usually related to satisfactory employment situations or financially successful entrepreneurship. It may also include highly idiosyncratic negative experience, such as pursuit by police authorities, an unsatisfactory marital union, or, on the other hand, the winning of a large prize in the Dominican national lottery.

A Typology of Commitment

Salient Factors	Status	
	Temporary	Permanent
	NO COMMITMENT	
Visa status	non-immigrant, tourist (illegal)	immigrant
Social and economic factors	primary kin remain or ownership of re- sources in D. R.	primary kin in N. Y. or ownership of house or business
Age and sex	older, or female who remains primarily within the household	younger persons or females with new social roles
Length of time in New York	new arrivals, retirees	extended New York residential experience
Experiential	low valued job, conflict with authorities, unacculturated.	highly valued job, facility with English, acculturated
		COMPLETE COMMITMENT

Sequential Development

Intimately connected with this typology of commitment is a sequential developmental pattern through which the immigrant typically progresses. How far the individual goes in this sequence is a function of the level of his commitment to remain in New York. Basically, it is possible to isolate four main temporal periods: initial enthusiasm and dependence; disillusionment; reluctant accommodation; retribalization.

The individual arrives with great enthusiasm and expectations, with a mixture of valid and invalid preconceptions about New York. In the beginning, immigration is seldom looked upon as more than a temporary sojourn to seek employment, to earn a stake. At the time of initial entry, the individual is extremely dependent upon others who are more experienced in finding housing and employment; persons

known to him from the village often mediate the discontinuities between cultural behavioral expectations of Santo Domingo and New
York. Any early problems of loneliness, frustration, or adjustment are
more than compensated for by the fact that in New York one is able
to earn sums of money impossible to achieve at home.

It is during this initial period that an immigrant most often holds
several jobs at once. Getting to New York involves borrowing $500 to
$1,500 at interest rates of up to six percent per month on an annual
basis. Quick repayment releases the individual from heavy economic
as well as moral obligations. The ability to remit money to parents,
wives, children, and even siblings is a fulfillment of a deeply socialized
sense of obligation. But this zeal to earn money also isolates them socially. It was during this period, many informants told me, that they
got jobs in *el campo,* in New Jersey or Long Island; suburban restaurants and clubs paid for overtime work and in some cases even
furnished living quarters. Even for those who remained in the city, the
time consumed by holding down two or more jobs left scarcely any
time for socializing with family or friends.

This then led to the second stage, a period of disillusionment,
loneliness, and deep frustration. Once the immediate need to repay
the loan is past, the individual begins to realize that in spite of hard
work, his savings are not as great as he had expected. The cost of living is higher than anticipated, the climate uncomfortable.* The assistance he has received to become established is no longer so generously given, as he is now expected to "scratch with his own nails"
(*arañar con su uñas propias*). At the same time, as a result of his experience in New York, his own level of expectation has moved higher.
Contact with a wide range of material items—clothing, telephones,
sufficient food, automobiles for some—and the perceived possibilities
of obtaining them make neither the old way nor the new situation
tenable. During this period of vacillation trips back to the Republic
are most frequent. Visits may last two to three months, and some migrants, especially older ones whose immediate family members have
remained in the village, stay permanently. Often the original decision
that only one person should go north is reversed and the remaining
wives or husbands and children are brought back to New York. It is
my distinct impression that the majority of those individuals who return permanently to the village after only a year or so in New York
do so because of illegal visa status. For most, visits to the village are

* The text of a *merengue* (a popular song form), *"El Esteem,"* is about a
strange New York disease that most Hispanos seem to catch. It is marked by dry-
ness of the throat, headaches, and coughing. The obvious cause is the low hu-
midity in steam-heated apartments, something that a person accustomed to a
tropical climate finds difficult to comprehend, hence the play on words.

only a temporary holiday and reinforce the realization that life in New York, whatever its trials, is the only viable *modus operandi*. They remain intent on continuing in New York only until they accumulate enough money to return permanently and successfully to the Republic. How long this takes depends upon specific objectives that are set and the vicissitudes of the New York experience. Short-term immigrants remain the least acculturated and assimilated segment of the Dominican population in New York.

Simon and Estella have been in New York four years. Their three children remain with Simon's mother near Santiago. He is intent on returning to buy back the land his father was forced to sell some years ago. Both Simon and Estella work in a plastic handbag factory. So intent is he on maximizing their savings that they live at a bare subsistence level, keeping household and personal expenses to a minimum. The apartment they rent is furnished only with chairs, a table, and beds. Rooms are rented out to a young single brother and a *compadre* who has a visitor's visa. Estella has six siblings living in New York, most of whom are openly critical of Simon's penurious *campesino* behavior. At first they were reluctant to introduce me to them because of what they felt to be the bad impression I might gain of the family seeing such "poor" people. Actually, in four years of New York residence, they have been able to accumulate over $11,000 in a savings account. In addition to his regular factory job, Simon occasionally works on weekends as a dishwasher in a major hotel.

The third stage is accommodation to rather than an acceptance of or assimilation into American culture and society. To some, accommodation represents little more than an uneasy truce sometimes expressed as being "caught in a trap." To others it is a series of selective adaptations of certain culture items and societal activities which are in Spicer's terminology "isolative" or "compartmentalized," a process which results in social and cultural "integration" rather than "assimilation" (1960). In this process culture traits are taken on so as to conform to the meaningful and functional relations within the individual's ongoing culture system rather than being accepted in terms of the new system. For example, one's valuation of personal success might well be made in terms of the remittances sent back to the village rather than in the public display of affluence that would come from moving to a suburb on Long Island. Work in a factory or even shift work in a restaurant requires conforming to rigid time requirements, a rigidity unnecessary in a rural situation. The compartmentalization of their lives into what one expressed as "giving the devil what he requires," that is, getting to work daily and on time, and then returning to the intimacy of the circle of *familia* and *amigos,* is learned early in the New York experience.

It is during this period that many perceive a futility in holding several jobs at the cost of attenuating personal relationships, and even becoming ill from the mental and physical strain involved.* For some, New York becomes a kind of purgatorial time that is to be accepted as their *suerte* (fate). They often express a belief in the futility of striving too hard, feeling they are not as clever as the Americans,** and that Hispanos, no matter how hard they work, are categorized as subordinate by the dominant *Americanos*.

Others during this stage make themselves as comfortable as possible, seeking employment situations which satisfy both the desire to be paid well and to be able to retain strong ties within their kin and friendship networks. Two variants of the latter are reflected in the actions of those who emphasize either the material and economic aspect or those who placed primary value on high levels of interaction with friends and kin.

Within a single house, but separate households, can be found examples of each of these variants. Pedro is an auto mechanic, a trade he learned in New York. His wife, a cousin, received a secondary education in Santiago, and in New York works as a secretary in a Spanish-speaking office. After four years in New York, Pedro and his wife saved enough money to buy a house with two rental units. Both worked diligently at remodeling and maintaining the house. They prided themselves for having dropped their *"campesino* way of thinking," and in their material acquisitions, but above all in acquiring a working knowledge of English. But in acquiring these things, it was necessary to spend much time away from their respective families. Saturday afternoon was spent in varnishing the floor, not in visiting.

Emilio was one of their renters. He worked as a custodian while his wife worked as a sewing-machine operator in a blouse factory. His work schedule allowed him to finish early in the afternoon. Almost every afternoon and early evening was spent in a round of visiting with other Dominicans in both Manhattan and Queens. These activities were not unremunerative since they placed him in a position to act as a broker in certain surreptitious activities such as selling lottery tickets and making arrangements involving visas. Their household reflected a style reminiscent of that found in a rural Dominican home. Spanish was spoken exclusively and the TV set and radio were invariably tuned to Spanish-speaking stations.

* Two individuals told of returning to the village for extended periods of time to recover from illnesses, evidentially the result of fatigue from overwork. The American Consul in Santo Domingo felt that this represented a significant problem among those who returned.

** Both in the Republic and New York one often hears Dominicans belittling their own technological knowledge. Americans are assumed not only to be rich but also extremely knowledgeable about technical and material things. The price, so this logic seems to go, is that Americans never possess that warmth in interpersonal relationships that is seen as an essential feature of the culture of *La Raza*.

However outwardly different these life styles may appear, both families see themselves primarily as Dominicans, more broadly as part of *La Raza*, but certainly not as Americans. Their vision of the future assumes a return to the Republic. It is their hope that their children, as native United States citizens, will be able to reap the material advantages of such citizenship without adopting the American frame of reference. This point of view is also reflected by almost all children reared primarily in New York who repeat this definition of their ideal life style. Thus, when they speak in terms of "my country" they are referring to Santo Domingo, not New York.° This allegiance was evidenced most poignantly by a 27-year-old man who had lived in New York six years. In this time he had learned to be a cutter in the garment industry, a relatively skilled and well-paying job. This affluence allowed him to acquire a standard of living that was considerably above that of many of his fellow villagers, as well as siblings, living in New York. Both he and his wife had learned functional English, lived in a well-furnished apartment complete with a wide assortment of expensive appliances, and drove a late-model convertible automobile. In a discussion, he asked rhetorically if it was right for him "to have left my country [the Dominican Republic] even for all this." Immediately after his father's death in 1970, he left New York with his entire family, returned to the village, and continued the operation of his father's small *bodega*.

A fourth phase of adjustment can be delineated for those individuals who, although they have not necessarily severed their links to Dominicans, have broadened their social network to include a great many Hispanos. It must be remembered that the very size of the Spanish-speaking population in New York has allowed for the development of a recognizable subcultural pattern, distinctive to the historical and ecological setting in which it has developed. Participation in this subculture involves far less relearning and transformation of the newly arrived Spanish-speaking immigrant's social and cultural norms than would be entailed in "becoming American" or more pejoratively, becoming a gringo (*agringado*).

In describing a similar phenomenon in urbanizing African states, the process has been labeled as retribalization as opposed to detribalization. While use of such terminology here is open to criticism for

° Dominican legal codes allow for dual citizenship even though United States law does not, a discrepancy that is perceived as a form of discrimination against Dominicans. According to the Dominican Consul in New York, a New York-born child of Dominican parents need only declare himself Dominican to be recognized as such. This act normally would deprive the individual of his American citizenship, but only if American authorities were aware of it. An individual acquiring United States citizenship through the process of naturalization technically remains a Dominican citizen.

possessing meanings not here intended, Cohen's definition of retribalization aptly describes what has happened in New York as disparate national groups of Spanish-speaking individuals emerge with a collectively conscious ethnic identity.

. . . an ethnic group adjusts to the new realities by reorganizing its own traditional customs, or by developing new customs under traditional symbols, often using traditional norms and ideologies to enhance its distinctiveness within the contemporary situation (1969:1).

The stage of social process considered here as retribalization carries with it the notion that the individual is capable of carrying out social roles that allow him to participate in both North American and Hispano social situations; I use it in preference to the rubric "biculturalism" because the latter implies a unidirectional culture shift. Few Aldeanos have at this point in time consciously reached this stage. The nearest examples are those I call culture brokers, exemplified by a travel agent. The rapidity with which retribalization takes place appears related to educational achievement, either in the Republic or in New York. The retribalization process is, however, taking place unconsciously and imperceptibly among most New York immigrants and is implicitly recognized by them when they describe the New York experience as having opened their eyes. Although seldom articulated by the younger Aldeanos who have been reared and schooled in New York, this identification with the core elements around which the retribalization process takes place is apparent.

A further example of retribalization is in styles of popular music among Hispanos. While at the broader national level American popular music tastes are led by styles of rock music to which listening in concert rather than dancing is the norm, New York Hispano teenagers are crowding into ballrooms and actively dancing to big brassy bands playing rhythmic Latin American-style music. The massive rock concerts which were so much a part of the American cultural experience of the late 1960's were parallelled by large audiences of Spanish-speaking young people, crowding Madison Square Garden for such attractions as Raphael, a Spanish singer whose passionate romantic style is reminiscent of popular American vocal styles of the 1950's.

CHAPTER SIX

Adaptations of Social Structures: Household, Marriage, and Role

The migration to New York of much of the village's population has had important repercussions on the traditional patterns of marriage, family structure, and role behavior of the participants in Aldea. At the same time, the migrants have carried most of these behavior patterns to New York, readapting them in response to social and economic demands of the new situation.

Residence

Neolocal residence is the Dominican norm for setting up new households at the time of the formation of a conjugal union, although often physical proximity to other kinsmen and patterns of frequent visitation make it difficult to perceive this. Migration has tended to negate this norm in both the village and New York. At present, a young couple in the village is almost invariably involved in the migration stream and, consequently, setting up a new independent household has little purpose. Rather, the individuals become part of an established unit. Typically, when one spouse and/or children remain behind, they reside with other kinsmen, most likely parents or a sibling. The migrant family members may set up a new household in New York after the majority of their nuclear family has arrived but initially at least, they are merely participants in an ongoing-unit. The new residence will undoubtedly be physically near other kinsmen.

Heads of Household

In the idealized family, the father is the *jefe*, the leader or head. He is traditionally seen as a stern, if not remote individual. If he should maintain other household units in concubinage, the fact, while public knowledge, seems not to be a topic of discussion within a family unit. When questioned about her husband's "outside" family, the legal wife of such an individual commented, "I try to look some other place or think of something else."

The degree of deference shown the father appears to be a function of his ability to provide for the family, which in turn is a reflection of his economic position, as well as of his willingness to perform the role expected of father. A comparison follows of two males in the village, both of whom have fathered large numbers of children in multiple unions.

Alfonso, a prosperous landowner, has fathered a total of 47 children within four unions that he has maintained concurrently throughout long portions of his adult life. All his progeny—22 either are currently or have been residents in New York—respected him fully and deferentially as their father. Among themselves they usually referred to one another as *hermano* or *hermana* regardless of the union from which they came. Because Alfonso was generally considered by the villagers to be a proper, trustworthy individual, who assumed the economic and social responsibility for properly rearing his many children, his fecundity is without any social stigma.

Roman, 45, is a subsistence agriculturalist who lives with his wife and three small children in an earthen floored *bohio*, one of the few houses in the village with neither water nor electricity. He has fathered an unknown number of children in previous unions which he no longer publicly recognizes. Romancito, one of these children who lives in New York, has no formal communication with his father. "I don't want to even remember he is my father. He never did anything for her [Romancito's mother] but give her babies." However, when Romancito's wife took their two children back to the village on a visit, she took them over to see their *abuelo* (grandfather) early in their stay.

A consequence of migration is that in the village the expected household head, the person who is the chief economic contributor and the unit's ultimate decision-maker, may be 1,500 miles away, returning only periodically for several weeks or months. In cases where the male is in New York, the female is left by default to make many decisions she would not ordinarily make, and to exercise power and carry out activities which traditional social norms dictate are not assigned to females.

In New York the household head may be the person, regardless of age or sex, chiefly responsible for the recruitment of other members and to whom the individuals owe obligations, both economic and moral. This person may well be the one who speaks the most functional English, commands the best economic resources, and has sufficient experience with New York life to assume a broker role for others. In many New York households the father is the person least able to perform these roles, especially if he has arrived as a mature adult saddled with the pressures and obligations to provide immediately for wife and children left behind. The new occupant of the head role may complain bitterly and express his desire to "get this load off my back." But when the opportunity arises for him to vacate the role —for example, those to whom he has been remitting money back in the village may arrive to assume occupational roles in New York—he rationalizes his continuation of such role behavior because of his sense of obligation.

Marital Unions

The term "marital union" has been deliberatly used in this context rather than "marriage" to distinguish between types of such social units. Although technically, "marriage" and "marital union" may be considered synonymous, the former implies the performance of certain legal and religious acts which entail obligations binding individuals so that dissolution is accomplished only through formal and public acts. A divorce, either from legal or sacred ties, no matter how easily obtained, still demands the participation and judgment of an outsider. A marital union merely implies common household inhabitation for a prolonged period by two individuals who engage in sexual activity which may lead to procreation of children and a line of descendants. Three types of stable marital unions must be recognized among Dominicans: *matrimonio por la iglesia* (ecclesiastically sanctioned marriage); *matrimonio por la ley* (civil marriage ceremony); *unión libre* (free union).

Both in the Dominican Republic and in the United States a marriage is considered legal if the ceremony is performed by any official sanctioned by the state to perform such acts. In the Republic the civil and religious aspects of this marital bond are recognized by the performance of two ceremonies, one by a civil authority and the other by an ecclesiastical representative. The Catholic Church makes divorce extremely difficult when a marriage has its sanction, and a civil ceremony alone satisfies legal requirements without entailing the moral obligations of permanent bonding that a religious ceremony does.

A *boda* (marriage ceremony) performed by a priest involves the expenditure of money for the attendant *fiesta* and, often, clothing for the occasion. For economy alone many do not seek such a ceremony. Of greater import is the fact that a marriage *por la iglesia* is considered irrevocable and many younger persons frankly admit they do not want such permanent ties. During my residence in Aldea only one such ceremony was performed and that by an elderly man of some means who formally acknowledged a free union of many years' standing. Religious ceremonies are much more typical of middle-class than *campesino* behavior. Several civil ceremonies were performed for Aldeanos during my stay in the village; one partner was a New York resident who was temporarily in the Republic.

Understanding the continuum of marital union types is essential to understanding the New York immigrant's behavior. These types accommodate United States legal requirements for securing a visa, yet express the norm of both serial and polygamous unions commonly practiced in the Dominican Republic. At the same time, by rationalizing polygamous unions they allow the immigrant to enjoy ongoing intimate familial relations in the Republic and the absence of sexual and social restraints in New York. Free unions, for example, are useful, socially recognized arrangements that allow living with a woman in New York, yet maintaining the legal spouse and nuclear family unit back in the village.

Because of the reluctance of most persons to make public declaration of their status it is difficult to estimate the number of marital unions in any single category. There is no doubt, however, that a higher percentage of unions formed among New York residents than among villagers is legally and/or ecclesiastically sanctioned. While most immigrants present illegally in the U.S. enter into temporary free unions if they form any kind of union, they may instead contract legal marriages in the hope that these will provide leverage in obtaining a valid residence visa, especially if children result from this union. Immigration law pressures individuals to form legally recognized unions in order to have a basis for sponsoring a spouse or children into the United States. This requirement can be met through civil ceremonies without, from the Dominican point of view, entering into the irrevocable contractual relationship of a marriage *por la iglesia*.

Since the religiously sanctioned marriage ceremony carries with it marks of higher socioeconomic status, a larger proportion of the long-term New York immigrants are willing and able to enter into such an arrangement. This is especially true of those who have achieved a degree of economic success and stability in their New York situation. Latorre (1969) has demonstrated in his sample of 356 families in Bonao, a provincial town in the Cibao, how the distribution of free unions to marriage (both civil and church unions) alters over a period of time, indicating a life-cycle pattern of early free unions, with more people entering into formal unions in their mature years. It is quite possible to posit that part of the reason the immigrant marries earlier in life is that in the migration experience the kind of economic and social prerequisites for formal marriage are fulfilled earlier.

A considerable body of anthropological and sociological literature exists on the nature of family patterning in the Caribbean. While these discussions provide much insight into the conceptualization of family and household forms, they are largely based on ethnographic data from British West Indian populations. A significant difference between them and the Dominican Republic is that social approval of concubinage and polygamy cuts across all levels of Dominican society rather than being limited to the lower classes. The impact of the migration to New York is to place the individual in a milieu that approves such activities far less, especially as upward social mobility takes place. In addition, the economic situation in New York is such that polygamous relationships are less feasible; as many commented, "It costs too much to support more than one family." On the other hand, the same economic situation makes keeper or consensual relationships even more desirable, especially when one or both participants are remitting money to the Republic to maintain family units in existence there.

The intricacies possible in civil and religious relations are illustrated in the case of a female who came to New York on a visa issued to her sister. Since her visa bore her sister's name, her marriage license was of necessity issued by New York authorities in that name. When she asked her priest to perform the ceremony he refused because he felt he could not marry her as long as the civil license did not bear her real name. She was forced to seek a civil ceremony.

ENDOGAMY

In the village the majority of marital unions are formed endogamously with others from the same immediate area. Marriage to first cousins, even though forbidden by Dominican law is frequent, although not necessarily valued in itself. Given the size of extended family units and the number of children fathered by a typical male, most people with whom an individual socializes can trace kinship links to one another. In the absence of an incest rule forbidding such unions, frequent cases of first-cousin marriages are to be expected. "Who else could I come to know when we spent most of our time visiting back and forth in our family? As a girl I had little chance to meet anyone outside my [extended] family," reported one woman who had married her first cousin when both first arrived in New York.

At least until recent changes, U.S. immigration law tended to encourage monogamous marriages, since it was easier to get an immigration visa if one had a marital relationship with a U.S. resident. A sizable number of these unions began as commitments of convenience between persons known to one another, and have since become permanent. Accepting such arrangements with complete outsiders has many pitfalls, however.

Louis arrived in New York at the age of 15. Three years later he was contacted by a "friend," a travel agent, who offered him $500 plus travel expenses to go to the Republic and marry, for the purpose of obtaining a visa for his wife-to-be. For Louis, even though he held strong religious convictions, the arrangement was ideal as it was an opportunity to earn a holiday at home. He traveled to the Republic, married the girl in a civil ceremony, and signed the necessary immigration forms. Aside from several meetings to sign papers concerning his "wife's" arrival, he had no further contact with anybody concerning her. She came and lived "somewhere in Long Island" but he claims never to have seen her. Two years later Louis decided he wanted to marry another Dominican girl but found that a divorce was necessary from the first wife, the expense of which he would have to bear. Since he had had no contact with her, he had to spend considerable time just locating her. The wife's elder brother, who had made the original payment, refused to come to his aid, explaining that the original amount was given to cover the cost of the divorce proceedings.

TABLE 8. MARITAL UNIONS OF ALDEANOS IN NEW YORK

	Number	Percent
Kinsmen	43	36
Others from Aldea area	36	31
Cibaenos	25	21
Other Dominicans	11	9
Other Hispanos	3	3
Total	118	100

Although the majority of the unions in the table above were formed prior to immigration, a sampling of legal unions that had been formed in 1969 in New York indicated that most Aldeanos still married Dominicans; however, a higher percentage of such unions were with individuals from outside the individual's geographic proximity or circle of kinsmanship.

PROCREATION

The desirability of procreating many children is a culture norm. Any discussion of how many a couple wants to have is usually shrugged off with *"Que Dios quiere"* ("What God desires"). During the long Trujillo regime, it was official policy in the Republic to promote a high birth rate with the rationale that insufficient population would leave the nation open to the threat of Haitian aggrandizement. It was not until late 1967 that the government officially recognized the need for population planning programs and openly supported family planning clinics. To date such programs have had limited impact and are concentrated in cities and towns *; in the village the topic was usually avoided. "Two topics I never touch are talking about forming cooperative associations [the failure of an earlier one had left much bitterness] and birth control. The men are afraid [under birth control] they won't be thought of as men and many of the women believe it causes sickness," said one of the priests serving the village. Actually, a good many women have learned about various birth control techniques from persons who have been in New York; some village women practice them. Although no data are available, it appears that the prolonged absence of husbands who have migrated to New York results in fewer birth among the females who remain behind.

In New York, while males continue to denounce birth control measures and speak of the desirability of procreating large numbers of children, there is a marked contrast between the number of children born to siblings living in the Republic and those living in New York. It is obvious that those remaining in the Republic have continued to have children in large numbers, while movement to New York has evidently severely restricted childbearing rates. This does not necessarily mean that the lower birth rate is the result of a change of attitude about the ideal size of a family. Most informants recognize the economic limitations of rearing children in New York—housing, food, and clothing are expensive there. For some, an important consideration is that children limit the mother's ability to work. While both husband and wife may limit the number of children they have their motives for doing so may be dissimilar. The ability of a wife to contribute to the total household income is desirable from a male viewpoint, but employability also provides the female with an independence and social identity she would have no opportunity to express were she responsible for children. For some women, this latter reason is consciously articulated: "I can buy things I want without having to wait for him to give me money. . . . He may find another girlfriend and I won't have to depend on him."

There are several ways to avoid child care responsibilities and still continue working, but these work best when the number of children is small. Bringing a parent from the Republic to carry out the custodial function is one, sending the children to the village or leaving

---

* For a discussion of the history of these programs and the relationship between the Catholic Church and the government over the issue of birth control, see Ortega, 1971.

them there is another. In some cases a sister, sister-in-law, or *comadre* living nearby in a separate household may assume this obligation while the mother works.

I first met Clotilde, 20, in the village when she arrived from New York with her two small children whom she had brought to leave with her husband's mother (her own mother was living and working in New York). One of the children became ill shortly after arrival and the Dominican physician counseled her to return immediately to New York with the sick child. This she did, leaving her son behind. Later in New York the presence of the daughter and absence of the son was a constant concern to the parents who then brought the boy back. However, after one month in the household, the problems of finding acceptable care for two children while the mother worked forced the decision to send both children back to the village. A habitual form of jesting between husband and wife was that she had become pregnant. When she actually found herself pregnant, she induced an abortion.

EMPHASIS ON VIRGINITY

It is important to all Dominican males that a prospective bride be a virgin. Premarital and extramarital sexual experience for males is not only tolerated but expected, but parents go to great lengths to protect their daughters from participation in any sexual experience, partly for fear of ruining marriage possibilities. Girls, therefore, are considerably more restricted in social relations outside the household than are their brothers. A father of six small children, all born in New York, said:

I try to teach my children what I know of the right and wrong ways to act. I want them to have respect for God, the name of their family and their mother. If the boys do not, I am sorry and maybe have not been a good father. But the girls . . . I must be careful for them. After all, if they should do something bad, who would want them [as wives]? I know you Americans do not think that way, but I am a Dominican and so are my children.

The above informant had a brother whose oldest children were in their late teens. The oldest son in this family was literally kicked out of the household when he repeatedly was a truant, used alcohol— his father suspected drugs—and "came in with those red marks on his neck."

I told him, you can get out. You want to act like a man and not listen to your father, then go. What about the younger ones when they see and know you do such things. You can still be a man, but what about your sister [aged seventeen]? What happens when she does something bad? No one will ever marry her. I can't tell her to leave like I can you.

One reason for the frequency of early marriage of girls in New York and in the village is that at the age of fifteen or sixteen they are assumed not to have had time for sexual experience. This concern for virginity also expresses itself in humorous references in male conversation.

When adolescent Dominicans attending school in New York discussed personal problems with me, girls almost invariably spoke about the overprotectiveness of their families and the elaborate ruses devised to escape their ever-watchful eyes. A frequent criticism by parents of life in New York dealt with this issue of children expecting to be loosened from tight parental control, and consequent failure to follow idealized Dominican norms of respect; disrespect was equated with "being an American." For girls this behavior was assumed to lead to a loss of virginity. For some of these girls, a sexual union represents the only route of liberation, even if the union is one of concubinage.

Maria, seventeen, a senior in a public high school, has been a successful student in New York schools for five years. She formed a free union with a newly arrived cousin with the consent of her parents. "My father always bugged me about my going out with boys and I could never do anything. By being married—she never openly admitted the illegal status of their union to me although her husband did—I can do more things now without him [her father] worrying if I will remain a young lady [virgin]."

It was undoubtedly the assumption of her parents that eventually the marriage would be legally consumated. In this particular case the union broke up after about a year, primarily because Maria was chronically ill and could neither contribute economically nor have children.

Sex Role Differentiation

Significant sex-role differentiation exists along urban-rural gradients as well as along class lines. In activities such as the preparation and serving of food, or the entertainment of guests, for example, the rural couple often shares more evenly the responsibility than do urban couples. However, the universal norm is that the male occupies the position of authority if he chooses to exercise it. Numerous subtle ways are open for the female to exercise a voice in or even a veto of the male decision but publicly, at least, the image of father or husband as the household authority figure must be maintained.

Although no female ever described herself as the decision-maker in the household, several were observed in this role. Latorre relates the incident in Mao when one of his Dominican field-workers "arrived at a house and asked who was the head of the family, the wife answered, saying in front of the husband: 'Well, the head of the family is this one, but here I am the one who gives the orders.' The husband looked dejected but never said a word" (1969:30). On a number of occasions, in interviews in households where I was not previously known, the husband began as the respondent, but deferred to his wife for her decision as to how complete and frank his answers should be.

Authoritarianism on the part of the male is marked. A frequent comment made by social service personnel who work with Spanish-speaking families is the contrast between Dominican and Puerto Rican males in the degree of strictness that the Dominican father maintains. As a result of this role expectation, the quality and tenor of the relations in father-child and mother-child dyads are markedly different. Whereas the mother fondles and overtly displays affection to her child, and this relationship is reciprocated, the father, especially during late childhood, withdraws any physical contact and is perceived as someone to be obeyed, if not feared. For some informants at least, the relationship was also remembered for a shift during adolescence from formal respect for the father to contempt, with the recognition that the father had loyalty to several family units. Even when the father-child relationship is not strained, the difference between mother-child and father-child relationships is best exemplified by the distinction between love and respect.

A typical mode of behavior on the part of the father to the child is one of teasing. This may include actions such as holding a wanted bottle just out of the infant's reach or holding a small child high overhead until he screams in fright. The cycle terminates with the child receiving what he wants, sometimes accompanied by a kiss or affectionate fondling.

While swimming with a father and his eight-year-old son, I noted the father insisted that his son should accompany him into deeper water inspite of pleas of "No, poppy." Once out into deep water the father refused to support his son, in order "to teach him to swim." He finally grabbed and held his son up after the boy had gone under and come up screaming, but made no attempt to comfort him. He laughingly took him to the bank where the son ran to be comforted by his mother. She hushed him but made no negative remarks about her husband's behavior.

If the father is ideally recognized with a distant, formal respect, then the mother is perceived as the source of love and affection. A direct parallel of this is found in the religious symbolism in which God the Father is seen as a stern demanding adjudicator, but Mary is the loving mediator. Scarcely a household does not contain a large picture of the Madonna with a gold heart shining in her bosom, even though there are seldom any other religious objects and symbols visible. Mother's Day is one of. the two times of year when the flow of remittances is greatest, and prices in the black market money exchange are highest, reflecting the demand for foreign exchange to pay for imported gift items.

The sharp dichotomy of sex roles begins early in life. For example, female babies are rarely allowed to be unclothed; body covering for male children is not nearly so important. Among the very poor in both rural and urban settings, small boys playing naked in the street are a usual sight and such nudity is seen as a class marker, something characteristic of *los pobres*. This nudity ceases at about the age of six and there are then strong prohibitions regarding public display of the unclad body. The fondling of genitalia on the part of male children is seldom reproved and continues as unconscious behavior into adulthood. Hispano males in New York are sometimes thought by Americans to be demonstrating their highly sexual orientation when they scratch or manipulate their genitals in public. Actually, they are unconscious of their acts and even of the general American norm against such actions. A male child's genitals are the subject of joking comments and jesting as to his future manliness. Such overt comments concerning a female child would be considered out of place. A girl child is elaborately dressed and groomed with highly ruffled dresses; during the first year her ears are pierced and earrings become an essential part of the female dress. At the same time, charm bracelets decorate the baby's wrist and chains with religious pendants hung about her neck. While bands of male children are allowed a good deal of freedom of movement, girls are much more carefully chaperoned and remain close at home, both in the village and in New York.

Socialization Practices for Family Interdependence

Loyalty to one's family grouping is imprinted early in a child's value system in a variety of ways. This bonding of relationships between family members is the result of a number of child rearing practices evident in the village and in New York. The large size of household units necessitates a great deal of interdependence and cooperation among the participants. The kind of privacy engendered by the American ideal of separate sleeping arrangements is impossible to obtain—even if it were desired—in either the simple small houses of the village or the small apartments of New York. A married couple and their five children can live ordered and remarkably well-adjusted lives in a three-room apartment if privacy is not the primary norm. The kind of interpersonal accommodation that is essential in such situations need not inspire either openly expressed tension or friction between the actors; rather it may serve to strengthen familial ties and solidarity.

Typically, especially in a crowded New York flat, children are given little opportunity to be alone. There are relatively few material possessions in even well-to-do Dominican households, and a child's play objects are much more likely to be other people than objects. The learning processes involved in handling toys that an American child is typically exposed to is by and large absent for a Dominican. In the village one of the very few non-American toys I observed was a *carrito,* a crudely made scooter, whose essential parts were a block of wood and wheels made from the hard disk-shaped nut of the *havilla* tree. Dolls and toy cars, rubber balls and games, when present at all, were usually gifts of someone who had returned from New York. This dearth of toy play objects is also noticeable among New York residents.

Responsibility for rearing a child typically lies not only in the nuclear family, but in the extended family, including fictive kinsmen, as well. The migration process increases the probability that a child will have to live with a variety of individuals, especially at the beginning of a family's exodus to New York. He may be left behind while one or both parents journey to New York to establish a household. This period may be very brief or it may last for years. In other cases the child may shuttle back and forth between the village and New York as the circumstances of the family change. In New York there is every probability that at least a portion of early childhood will be spent in the daytime care of another while his mother works or that his family circle will be enlarged as his mother cares for someone else's child.

Until adolescence, play group participants tend to be mixed in age, in part because children are expected to assume responsibility for younger siblings.

My frequent companions in the village were nine-year-old Felipe and his five-year-old brother, Niño. The large play group that often assembled in the church yard was undifferentiated as to age or grade level. Participation was limited only by the degree of maturation necessary to perform the acts required in events at hand. Marble shooting occupied much time, and only Niño's lack of coordination, and subsequent quick loss of his marbles, prevented his participation. During these play periods, Felipe never allowed Niño to escape his attention. Whenever his smaller brother started wandering off from the group, he was recalled by Felipe. To a lesser degree the two boys assumed responsibility for their three-year-old sister whenever they remained around the house. Adolescent boys assumed far less of this kind of responsibility than their sisters, but it was not uncommon to see them holding a younger sibling in their arms while engaged in a street conversation with members of their own age set.

In a crowded New York apartment it is difficult to avoid interaction with siblings, especially since parents are reluctant to allow their children to be on the street. This deeply socialized practice of continual interaction with others results in adults who find isolation for any length of time difficult to accept. This partially accounts for employment and residence patterns. The theme of loneliness and isolation is common in discussions with those who accept employment where other Hispanos are not present, or who have attempted to move to areas, even inside the city, that do not allow for considerable interaction with other Spanish-speaking individuals.

SOCIAL ROLE TRANSFORMATION

The migration to New York has repercussions on traditional sex-role relationships as social roles are redefined in the new ecological setting. New York provides an opportunity for females to emerge from the traditional pattern of male dominance. The female often finds herself equally, if not more, employable than the male, especially in the garment industry or in light factory work. Her financial contributions often become important, if not essential, to the attainment of family goals. If the end sought is merely the maximum accumulation of capital for the family's return to the Republic, her resources become vital.

Emillo and Clotilde both were employed and arranged for the care of their three small school-aged children with a relative in the same apartment building. Emillo's plastics factory job was terminated and for a while he awaited another opening in the factory while drawing unemployment insurance benefits. During this time he also became super of his apartment building, and when the insurance funds ceased, it was decided that he would remain at home caring for the children and carrying out his building maintenance job. He was at first somewhat uncomfortable in this new role definition and jested about it saying that he had now "really become an American." Meanwhile, his wife, who had always earned more as a garment worker than he did as a factory laborer, continued to work at her job. In commenting on her situation she said, "In Santo Domingo [the village] I could have hired someone to help me in the house and with the children, but I still like it better here when I am earning money."

However, in other situations the tendency is for the new situation to reinforce traditional modes of behavior. This is especially so when the female stays at home caring for children. She has little, if any, contact with American culture, and rarely learns English. Consequently, she becomes more subservient and deferential to her husband's wishes and decisions, especially when they concern relationships outside the family. Traditional norms require that a proper lady not be seen alone on the streets and, therefore, remaining close to home reinforces these norms.

Eva, the wife of Maximo, has lived for twelve years in New York but has always remained at home caring for their six children. She has no knowledge of English and very seldom ventures outside her tenement apartment without being accompanied by her English-speaking husband or children. Because of concern over the possible robbery of the apartment, one adult is almost invariably present. With the exception of occasional trips to a *bodega* nearby, she is absolutely dependent upon her husband or the older children to do all the shopping. Within the family circle she carries considerable voice as to decisions that are made, but in all outside relations she is completely dependent on her husband, and to some extent on her English-speaking children. Spanish is the exclusive language of the home because Maximo says, "I want my wife to know everything that is going on, what they [the children] speak outside, I can't control."

The role of the child is also changed in the new situation as he or she learns English and becomes better equipped to cope with life in New York. In many ways the child becomes the culture broker for the family as his language fluency and experience place him in pivotal roles in dealing with the wider society. It is he who helps fill out English-language forms, answers the door and telephone when an *"Americano"* is involved, and in general interprets the outside world to his elders, often manipulating the situation to his advantage.

CHAPTER SEVEN

Non-kin Activities

In the preceding chapter we considered the impact immigration has had upon those aspects of social organization which base membership primarily upon kinship ties. We turn now to an examination of some social features arising from extra-familial relationships: voluntary associations, the structural relationship of the immigrant to formally constituted institutions of authority, and the emergence of the travel agent as a culture broker.

Voluntary Associations

Voluntary association activities, that is, "formally constituted groups bound primarily by ties of shared interest rather than kinship or coresidence" (Anderson 1971:219) among Dominicans in New York have a variety of stated purposes for their existence: social, political, economic, recreational, and religious. Their underlying functional significance for the participants, however, is seen to be often somewhat divergent from their stated intent. At the same time, it can be demonstrated that most of these activities have little or no appeal to the *campesino* immigrant from Aldea.

The use of voluntary associations, especially those regionally or tribally based, as one important adjustive mechanism in the new environment is an often noted social feature of immigrant behavior. [In the U.S. (Handlin 1959); in Egypt (Abu-Lughod 1967); in West Africa (Little 1965); in Mali (Meillassoux 1968); in Lima, Peru (Doughty 1970).] Little, examining such associations in West Africa, was concerned with developing a model by which the social transition from tribal to urban society (subsistence to market economy) could be partially explained. He demonstrated how these associations provide links between old and new role behavior and class structure, prerequisites to this transition. In a similar, if less structural, manner Doughty sees the integrative function of these associations.

. . . the situation facing the individual migrant in Peru is complex, and one must be startled *not* by the fact that there is apparent social chaos and anomie at times, but that so many individuals and families are indeed able to retain their integrative structures or to reorganize their lives in meaningful ways. One of the mechanisms by which this is accomplished is through associations whose basic criterion for membership is the peoples' common place of origin (1970:32).

In New York City one need only observe the speaking schedule of a political aspirant as he appeals for the votes of various ethnic segments to see how numerous such ethnically based clubs, unions, lodges and societies are. But the functional purpose that these groups serve has rarely been investigated. One observation on the difficulties experienced by the Puerto Rican population in assimilation to mainland life concerns this group's inability to organize itself along geocultural lines (Sexton 1965). That such a criticism is no longer valid, if it ever was, is apparent when one examines the emergence of such organizations as ASPIRA, The Young Lords, or the much more broadly based Puerto Rican Day Parade Association.

If one were to rely upon newspaper accounts, radio announcements and publicly posted information of Dominican associational activities, one could conclude that a similar social process is taking place among this group of foreign nationals. However, a closer examination of these groups, their reasons for being, leadership, and membership indicates they more often are instrumental in providing a basis for continued linkages to the Dominican Republic than in providing a basis for integration into life in New York. Their lack of either widespread appeal or success is often due to their concern with divisive political issues and candidates in the Dominican Republic, and their blatant use as instruments for personal aggrandizement. In many ways their image is such that most Dominicans are fearful of participating in any such organized activities.

The majority of these groups are overtly political, concerned with events in the Republic, promoting a particular Dominican political party or figure, or concerned with political-ideological issues in that country. Others, masquerading as purely social groups, are frequently just as politically oriented as those calling themselves political. Still others merely provide individuals and groups with a basis to personally profit by the activities of the club, or provide legitimated positions from which the organizer(s) may receive public attention.

Señora Jimenez Iturbides arrived as a political refugee in 1960 after her husband had been killed by Trujillo forces. She currently operates a small travel agency and translation office. Several years ago she organized a charitable organization, *Amigos de los Dominicanos,* which she serves as president and treasurer. Annually the group holds a benefit dinner charging as much as $15 a plate, the participants drawn primarily from the upper middle class Dominicans living in New York, many of whom are distantly related to her or her deceased husband. The planning and publicity involved in this activity gains her much publicity in the Spanish-language press, radio and television, as well as in the Dominican press. (The New York writer of Dominican affairs for one Spanish newspaper is also correspondent to one of the leading papers in Santo Domingo.) She personally takes the profits derived from these charitable events to Santo Domingo for distribution among her self-determined recipient charities. A similar organization, The Dominican Charitable Friends, has a broader based sponsoring group, but operates in essentially the same manner. Each charges the other with personally deriving profit (publicity as well as money) from their respective activities.

While these groups cater to rather elite segments of the New York colony, similar activities can be found at other social levels. One patriotic group made up of fewer than 20 members, and according to some, unwilling to add new members or hold new elections, often can be found attempting to represent *la communidad dominicana en Nueva York*, making public proclamations in its name. The emergence of this group of what some cynically view as opportunists is partly a result of the constant search by the dominant society for representatives of national categories of immigrants rather than specific organized groups. To whom does the Mayor's office turn to present the annual proclamation of Dominican Friendship Day? In this case, at least, it frequently is to whoever comes forward and presents himself as a representative.

Some individuals, such as political emigres in New York, envision being able to repeat the success of President Balaguer who, in his three-year period of political eclipse following his ouster in 1962, lived in New York, building a political base for his reelection following the revolution in 1965 (*The New York Times*, May 19, 1970).

Licenciado Ubaldo Cepeda was an active government supporter as a teenager during the Trujillo era and fled following his downfall. He is a graduate in law from the university in Santo Domingo, and continues to use his title in New York although he is not allowed to practice law here; he works for a shipping agency. Shortly after arriving in the U.S., he joined the army and served in Korea. After returning to New York he organized a small group of *Veteranos Dominicanos*, which gave him a basis for publicity. During the Dominican election campaign of 1970 he spoke out early in favor of one popular candidate and attempted to build a Reconciliation Party in New York. Unfortunately, his candidate died prior to the election and he was left with no feasible candidate to support. The majority of his political activity funds came from an arrangement with a mid-town restaurant that caters to Dominican dances: he receives a percentage for acting as broker and recruiter between the management and various Dominican groups. In addition, this activity provides him with many contacts with Dominicans who need the personal kind of broker services, translations, and visa arrangements which he provides for a fee.

Both *El Diario* and *El Tiempo*, the two major Spanish-language dailies printed in New York, carry full-page sections devoted to events and items of interest about Dominicans. In addition, the regular news columns present longer news stories of Dominican-oriented events. During the months preceding the 1970 Dominican Presidential election, these pages and news stories were almost completely devoted to the pronouncements, charges, and countercharges of political groups. At least twelve New York-based groups identifying themselves as separate political parties were identified in these pages, but the majority of them were exceedingly small and some represented only a momentary splitting from an established group. The arrival of a popular Dominican political figure in New York usually culminated in a fund-raising *cena* or *baile* (dinner dance) often attracting hundreds of persons. Immediately following these events, the organizing group retracted to its small nucleus of membership. Although U.S. immigration law forbids foreign citizens to engage in any political activity, little restraint seems to be exercised by INS officials. "We keep an eye on what's going on and sometimes have to remind them of the law," commented one official. One of the frequently discussed goals of these groups is to gain for New York residents the right to vote in Dominican elections. (At present, Colombia makes such a concession to its citizens living abroad, allowing them to cast their ballot in the offices of the Colombian consulate at the time of elections.)

Another type of organization is that devoted to the promotion of Dominican cultural events, sponsoring such activities as a recital of a Dominican pianist composer, the public exhibition of a Dominican painter, a poetry reading by a Dominican elocutionist, or the memorial activities surrounding a national holiday. The membership of such groups is small and usually restricted to persons from the Dominican urban middle class. The events they sponsor do, however, attract audiences of many hundreds drawn from the same social segment. The sponsoring groups receive much personal publicity, whatever their motives. At the same time, there is considerable factionalism involved among this elite group, part of it politically motivated. The removal of the New York Dominican Consul General from office in 1969 was accompanied by a shift in alignment within these groups (*El Diario*, August 29, 1969).

Attempts have been made to organize societies specifically dedicated to mutual aid of New York residents, but their inability to divorce themselves from either political machinations or personal aggrandizement has led to their rapid demise. The *Juventud Obreros Cristianos* (JOC), Young Christian Workers, with proclaimed goals of aiding all Spanish-speaking youth by helping them develop employment, language, and social skills in a Catholic setting, never developed an effective program and foundered when the Church withdrew its support. Part of the difficulty was that the leadership was taken over by Dominicans and other national groups dropped out. The Church, through JOC, funded English language instruction for the salaried leaders who, after this instruction, found better-paying jobs and dropped out of active leadership in the movement. The selective process of recruitment of participants from persons already known to one another, if not kinsmen, contributed to the development of a cliquish membership. New recruits were most often JOC activists in Santo Domingo who found in the New York group mutual acquaintances from former times, including those who had actively participated in the 1965 Revolution, or friends of friends. Both its socialistic and Catholic basis and the social action stemming from these bases were anathema to many Dominicans, and consequently JOC's appeal was never very wide. Rather than providing an opportunity for an integration of old and new role behaviors for most of its members, it made the reinforcement of old behaviors possible. Even for the handful of members who had lived in New York for most of their lives, it established a social identity linking them closer than ever to the Dominican Republic.

I observed two attempts by individuals to organize programs of aid to their countrymen which endured for only one meeting. A public call was made for a meeting of *El Grupo* for persons wishing to form an association to assist fellow Dominicans in New York. Over 30 persons, most known to one another, attended. Lengthy discussions at the meeting concerned various problems faced by their countrymen, and many critical remarks about U.S. immigration law and its enforcers were made. Repeated admonitions were made to keep the incipient organization apolitical. Finally, the almost predictable call to affiliation with a politically oriented Washington-based Dominican priest resulted in no decision and the group adjourned, vowing to meet again, and at that time to be genuinely apolitical. A subsequent meeting was never called, partly because some of the organizers returned to the Dominican Republic. The degree of nonpolitical orientation was, however, revealed through an invitation to me by one participant after the meeting's adjournment, to attend a fund-raising dance of the *Confederación Autónoma Sindicatos Cristianos* (CASC), a socialist-oriented Catholic political party. The majority of the participants in the earlier meeting were present at this blatantly political dance.

Another announced attempt to initiate an organization aimed at helping Dominicans in New York was made by Señora Fernandez, a middle-class Cibaena, who had lived in New York since 1940. Presently living in public housing, she has become active in numerous civil rights and poverty groups. Her fluency in both English and Spanish has provided her with numerous opportunities to serve as translator and go-between in the activities of local organizations, as well as giving her a sophistication about the politics and economics of poverty programs. In printed flyers distributed in housing projects and the heavily Dominican neighborhood on the West Side, she publicized an organizational meeting to discuss her proposal for a Dominican-American association aimed at helping Dominicans through English instruction and vocational training. This was to be underwritten by publicly funded poverty agencies to which she planned to apply for funds. The initial meeting attracted about 40 individuals. After first outlining her plan at length, she then opened the floor to discussion. Almost immediately chaos broke out as one individual placed the problems of Dominicans at the feet of U.S. imperialism and its support of Trujillo. Attempts by the chairman to focus attention back to her own plan were futile. For the most part, remarks centered about issues in the upcoming Dominican presidential election. One eloquent and emotional plea suggested the group could be used to give special classes for children on Dominican history and culture: "The children don't even know who Duarte is." (Duarte is honored as the founder of the Republic.) If any consensus was reached it was that Dominicans are a people wronged by U.S. employers, bureaucracy, and government policy, and that a redress of grievances was overdue. However, useful as it was as an opportunity to vent emotions, the meeting produced no further action. In a subsequent interview, the organizer expressed her bitterness that "My people don't know how to have a meeting, they know nothing about the rules." I suggested she might pool her ideas with another group (*El Grupo*) who also wanted to accomplish some of her objectives and had access to the nearby JOC meeting rooms. This suggestion was rejected outright; she said they were too political and would not want to follow her plan even though she claimed ignorance that the other group existed. A similar discussion with the organizer of *El Grupo* met with a statement that such a joint effort would never work. "We Dominicans are too jealous of one another." This remark of self-denigration was repeated by Dominicans in a variety of contexts.

But these overt public, social, and political activists represent a very small segment of the New York colony. Few persons when questioned in this area of activities admitted to membership or participation in any formally organized organization, and practically all positive responses concerned church-related activities. Among Aldeanos participation in formally organized activities was exclusively in the realm of church-sponsored activities.* A few admitted to earlier membership in political clubs but claimed rapid disillusion and withdrawal. "Shortly after I came to New York I got involved with some persons who said they wanted to work against the dictatorship of Balaguer. I wanted to help my country. But they were all thieves and liars. They just wanted to use you, your name, and your money."

The deep-seated fear and suspicion of public participation was illustrated when a *filial* (branch) of the PRD opened in Corona, Queens. The small building used as a local clubhouse had a large crudely painted sign saying *Partido Reformista Dominicano* on one outer wall. For most of its Dominican neighbors, the building was a source of embarrassment, and they asked, "Why must they bring their politics here?"

One of the few individuals from Aldea who attempted to participate openly in such formal political groups experienced the gamut of sanctions that his twelve siblings living in New York could mobilize. In spite of protests from his kinsmen, he joined a local PRD *filial* and was elected secretary. On occasion his name appeared in Spanish-language press news articles concerning activities of the *filial*. Various brothers and sisters attempted to get him to withdraw through appeals both verbal and written "to honor and not bring shame upon the family name." Eventually their economic sanctions compelled him to capitulate to their wishes. His salary of less than $100 per week barely supported his family of six growing children. The illness of one of his children forced him to turn to a brother for financial aid. The brother made withdrawal from political activity a condition of receiving aid. Two other brothers who own a prosperous *marketa* (grocery store) then offered him a job there at a salary greater than they probably would have paid to an outsider, and considerably more than he was then earning. Since the store hours included evening work, his ac-

---

* The Church as used here generally refers to the Roman Catholic Church. Among those persons I came to know both from the village as well as from other parts of the Republic, the Catholic Church was the only one attended. There are some Protestant evangelical congregations scattered about the city, including an extremely active and prosperous almost exclusively Dominican Seventh Day Adventist one on the West Side of Manhattan. It was originally begun as a general Spanish-speaking congregation, and it is interesting to note that within a short period of time, the Puerto Rican segment withdrew to participate in a church group of Puerto Ricans on the East Side.

ceptance of the job precluded further participation in the work of the party.

GROUP SAVING ACTIVITIES

The dependence upon activities made up of those in whom one places *confianza* is further illustrated by a savings practice common among families and friends. One method of collecting capital is through participation in an economic mutual aid group called a *san*. Several individuals agree to contribute a given sum at stated intervals, usually on a payday. The total amount collected at each interval is turned over to each person within the savings group in an order determined by drawing lots to spend as his own. The banker is normally the first to be given the money, in recognition of the task he performs in collecting from each member. In some versions used in the Dominican Republic the banker pays nothing each week into the pool; however, he is then held financially responsible for anyone who misses his payment.

Katzin (1959) reports a similar system called "partners" among Jamaicans and Herskovitz (1947) writes of *susu*, another version of the same thing, to be found in Trinidad. Kutzin notes that this form of savings group has been found among the Yoruba in Nigeria as well as among Peruvian Indians. I found a similar savings system called *pan* among West Indian immigrants in Puerto Plata, a north coast town in the Dominican Republic (Hendricks 1968).

While the arrangement appears to have little advantage over simple personal savings or borrowing from commercial loan agents, such a view assumes the availability of credit at less than exorbitant rates of interest. Many of the participants do not normally have access to public lending institutions, and their illegal immigrant status makes lending agents shy away from such loans. Experience in the Dominican Republic with the village *prestamistas*, even at his rate of six percent per month, makes many wary of getting involved with an impersonal finance company whose agents most often do not speak Spanish. Voluntary savings from a paycheck to accumulate surplus cash may be precluded by the demands on a paycheck of less than $100 per week, especially when it supports an entire family.

Obviously membership in such an extralegal group as a *san* is neither extended nor taken lightly. It is quite possible for an individual early on the list to take his "turn" and then refuse any further participation, leaving the remaining members minus the amount of his contribution. *San* groups are frequently organized within extended families and close friends for significant sums. In the largest reported

San eleven "participants" each contributed $100 every two weeks; a number of the eleven consisted of several members in a nuclear family or household contributing jointly. One person used the $1,000 he received when his "turn" came to bring up his four small children to New York. *San* is also played among employees well known to one another, including Anglo-Americans. However, the sums involved are much less and therefore less is at stake and risk taking is endured. The former kind of *san* group is usually saving for an express purpose for which large sums of capital are necessary while intentions of the latter are more frivolous. But the focus in any case is upon interpersonal relations rather than on impersonal unknown institutions such as banks.

BASEBALL

The national sport of the Dominican Republic, enjoyed almost to the exclusion of all others, is baseball. Certainly no urban area is without a number of local teams, and on the national level four leagues operate, playing a season which begins on October 24 and culminates in a national championship (*Serie Final*) playoff in late February. Daily newspapers devote considerable space to baseball news of both the Dominican Republic and the United States. Radio broadcasts relayed from the continent with Spanish-speaking announcers cover major league action, including the World Series. Dominicans follow with great national pride the exploits of their fellow countrymen who play on U.S. teams. In the 1969 season seventeen Dominican-born players, including such prominent players as Juan Marichal and the three Alou brothers, were signed with major league clubs.

In New York interest in baseball is further developed in young men through a variety of formally and informally organized teams and leagues that play in public parks under the auspices of private and public sponsors, the Schaeffer Brewing Company and the Police Precinct Community Relations units, for example. These teams and leagues take on a variety of forms but commonly tend to separate along broad ethnic lines; there are hundreds of teams made up exclusively of Spanish-speaking players. Sometimes teams are predominately Dominican, but this kind of segregation is more the product of recruitment of prospective players from among one's friends than any deliberate attempt to segregate nationalities. Membership in such teams provides the individual with socialization opportunities outside the restricted circle of family and previous friendship ties. Such activities are exclusively male and girls of the same age do not share in this opportunity for the extension of their contacts with the wider society.

In spite of the Dominican interest in baseball, there is no base-ball field in the village of Aldea and consequently few of the young men develop any proficiency at it. Only one of the village males that I came to know in New York participated as a player in this activity. They do, however, maintain a deep interest in it, listening to radio broadcasts and going to games at Shea Stadium, which is within walk-ing distance of the Dominican colony in Queens. From my observa-tions, it seems that with the exception of going to church, attending New York Mets baseball games is the public activity most often en-gaged in by those Aldeanos I knew in New York.

SOCIAL MOBILITY AND ASSOCIATIONAL ACTIVITIES

If the activities of most suprafamilial organizations serve so blat-antly to self-aggrandize the sponsors, one may ask why so many par-ticipate in the activities. For a large number it is a way of validating their social status vis-à-vis other Dominicans. A middle-class immi-grant accustomed to deference in his home country because of his family name or social position is unlikely to find it when participating in the general social milieu in New York. This is especially true when, because of his lack of language skills or technical competence, he has been forced to accept a socioeconomic situation which he considers inferior relative to the larger society—a university trained lawyer working as a hospital orderly or the descendant of a Dominican presi-dent working on the assembly line of a light bulb factory are but two examples of this. In other cases such occasions provide the newly prosperous immigrant with a means to validate his social and economic mobility. However, use of these activities in such a manner is difficult. "Too many people remember [who and what you were]. . . . It is important to keep in contact. Besides, how else could they [read I] go to the Waldorf Astoria or Tavern-on-the-Green? They take home a swizzle stick and a napkin with those names printed on it and their friends know they have been there. The only other way a Dominican would have of going to such places would be to wash the dishes." Actually, Dominicans do wash dishes in such places but they are not of the socioeconomic level as those attending these functions.

The Dominican Republic is usually depicted as a deeply stratified society, the lines of demarcation based upon family, money, and edu-cation (Roberts 1966:65). The rigidity of these lines and the social mobility that is possible is a debated issue (Lowenthal 1969). How-ever, a clear social cleavage exists between the rural peasant, the *campesino,* and those reared in an urban environment. With the rapid growth of urban areas, populated by former *campesinos,* the geographical distinction is no longer so rigid, and the term *campuno* is often used to denote an urbanized *campesino*. Although in a formal sense *campesino* simply refers to that class of individuals who are rural dwellers, it also carries the connotation of being a hick or hillbilly. The attributes commonly traced to the *campesino* complex include a distinctive uncultivated speech pattern, rude manners, lack of knowledge normally acquired through formal education, and a consequent naïveté. Accompanying the division between social classes is a great deal of ignorance of one segment about the life style of the other. The *campesino* is, undoubtedly with good reason, deeply suspicious of the city and its inhabitants, while the urbanite is contempuous of and condescending toward the *campesino*.

This social separation has been transferred nearly totally intact to New York.* Even here the *campesino* retains an awareness of his identity, and vacillates from embarrassment to pride in this identification. He seldom attempts or is allowed to enter the social world of his urban compatriots, much less those from the middle class, even though they may all work side by side in a New York factory. The recency of their migration has not allowed them to view themselves or others except through the social perspective of their own country. The continuous arrival of new recruits reinforces such views even though over time the bases shift and social linkages supporting them might be expected to become attenuated.

As their social network begins to go beyond the restricted pool of Aldeanos or even Cibaenos, friends are most likely to be other Latin-Americans of their own socioeconomic level: Colombians, Venezuelans, Mexicans, Cubans, and to a lesser extent, Puerto Ricans. Then if upward mobility takes place, it is within the larger context of the Hispano population, not among either Dominicans or *Americanos*. This is partially explained by the fact that these outsiders are far enough outside the Dominican experience to be unable to perceive the subtle class differences that a native culture bearer does. It may be that these new acquaintances find themselves in the same structural position in relation to the dominant American culture. At the same time, their common Hispanic cultural tradition and language allows for an ease of communication and mutual understanding that is not possible with *Americanos*.

* Among the New York population one can find Dominicans from all levels of society. Oscar de La Renta, whose fashion designs are pace setters in the female high fashion industry, is part of New York's most fashionable society. A number of Dominican physicians have extensive practices in the New York area. The concert master of the New York Philharmonic is from Santo Domingo.

Church

Although the people from Aldea remain quite separate from any of the previously discussed political or social organizations, they do participate in the activities of the Catholic Church with equal if not greater frequency than they did in the village. There the Church was the center of organized activity and it is not surprising that they seek out the same kind of associational center in New York. Regular participation in familiar, ritualized behavior is reassuring in an environment where so much is strange and incomprehensible. The weekly assemblage at mass facilitates the encounter with familiar persons who would otherwise not be seen.

In the village the priest is known as one of the few individuals beside kinsmen in whom one can place trust. Even though the village priest may be criticized for his "pushiness" in attempting to develop community school and health facilities, or the subject of ridicule as a *pajero* (masturbater) for his vow of chastity, the norm is still deeply held that he is a *persona de confianza.* At the same time he is a kind of *patrón,* one who serves as intermediary between the villagers and the authorities (both secular and sacred). Initially at least, the New York immigrant ascribes the same role behavior to the parish priest, who may or may not conform to this ideal. However, the presence of the priest, while desirable, is not essential to the religious ritual experience of these people. Petitions can be as easily aimed by the individual at saints or symbolic objects to act as intermediaries on behalf of the petitioners. The priest is not needed to act as intermediary. When the Church or its representatives in New York cannot or will not carry out expected personalistic acts for the members of the parish, the ritualized behavior of mass attendance persists since the religious experience is not dependent upon the clergy.

The arrival of large numbers of Puerto Rican Catholics in New York in the 1940's forced upon the Catholic hierarchy a basic decision of how these newcomers could best be incorporated and assisted (Fitzpatrick 1968:10). Historically, other immigrant groups had formed their own ethnic congregations, served by native clergy brought from the home country, but it was decided that it was neither economic nor practical to allow the Puerto Ricans to develop along these lines. Puerto Rico had historically lacked native clergy, and the Church had found it necessary to import foreign clergymen to serve its churches there. At this time a nucleus of trained native priests was being developed and the island could ill afford to export any to accompany the New York migrants. In addition, the Puerto Rico immigrants became replacement populations for existing ethnic groups and could easily use church facilities already in existence. (East Harlem, now known as *el Barrio,* was the home of a largely Catholic Italian population prior to the Puerto Rican influx.) The decision was made to use existing facilities and clergy to minister to the growing Spanish-speaking population in an integrated setting. The decision was built upon immediate logistical expedience and upon the premise that the Church could be more instrumental in integrating the newcomers into American life by integrating its own activities. During this period, it must be remembered, the "melting pot" concept of American society was still largely unquestioned.

The Roman Catholic churches serving the two largest concentrations of Aldeanos in New York represent sharp contrasts in their treatment of Hispano parishioners. Yet each Sunday both hold Spanish-language masses which overflow their large edifices.

In Corona the parish has seen successive waves of immigrants. First came Germans, followed by Irish, then Italians. The influx to the area of non-Catholic Negroes in the post-World War II period was paralleled by a decline in the activity and prosperity of the parish and its school. The present pastor is of Irish descent and claims to have been assigned to the parish because of a career of successful resuscitation of financially faltering parishes. Although no ethnic census is available, Father O'Hara estimated that at least half his parish is Spanish speaking, primarily from the Dominican Republic and South America. He is assisted by a Spanish priest who speaks little English. It is Father O'Hara's conviction that the Hispanos must learn American ways, including the English language, just as have previous immigrant groups. He is concerned about the limited financial contribution made by the Hispanos and believes that it is his job to teach them to give more generously. "The Italian peasants were very much the same way and we just had to teach them. Now if it weren't for them [the Italian parishioners] we couldn't pay our bills. But the Dominicans send so much back home or are saving for their own return and it is hard to get them to contribute their share to the parish. I know that they have it because they are Johnny-on-the-spot paying the tuition of their children in the school."

Even though the Spanish-language mass is filled to overflowing each Sunday, Father O'Hara declines to allow an additional mass, reasoning, "They will have to come to the English mass then." In the same manner he has been reluctant to allow the development of *cursillos* or *Legión de María* groups catering exclusively to Spanish speakers. A few militant middle-class Dominican youths (not from the village) attempted to organize a *Juventud Obrera Cristiana* cell among the younger parishioners; the pastor was somewhat intransigent. Insisting that one of the priests had to be presented at all meetings, he claimed the Spanish priest had no time available to attend JOC meetings. Padre Valdéz, the Spanish assistant priest, recognizes the conflicts within the congregation and expresses willingness to hold additional masses if permitted, but he cannot publicly oppose his superior. However, even though he speaks Spanish, there is a gap between his own culture and that of his Hispano parishioners and he is not averse to making perjorative remarks about the habits and customs of *campesinos*. The parish school has a number of Dominican children enrolled but will not accept anyone whose English facility is so limited that remedial or bilingual instruction is necessary.

In spite of the lack of enthusiasm shown by this parish toward the participation of large numbers of Spanish speakers in its activities,* their numbers continue to grow. The church's proximity is only part of the explanation, as there are other Catholic churches close by and in fact many of the weekly participants travel from far away in the Upper West Side and Brooklyn to be there. This church has become recognized as one of the points of weekly assemblage for families who are dispersed about the city.

In sharp contrast is the parish in Lower Manhattan, in the heart of what has been known as "Little Italy," which has also served waves of ethnic populations. The members of the parish have few middle-class pretentions. Upwardly mobile Italians have moved out, leaving behind their poor and unassimilated to inhabit the tenements; their empty apartments became the homes of many Dominican families from the Cibao. Two priests are assigned to the parish, one an Italian-born long-time U.S. resident, and the other Padre Jesús, a priest from Spain, one of several recruited some six years ago to serve the growing New York Hispano population.

Padre Jesús has developed close ties with his Spanish-speaking parishioners, especially the Dominicans. Following each Sunday's mass he holds a *cursillo* (literally a class of instruction; in reality a formalized gathering more social than religious in nature) in the parish hall. It is open to all Spanish speakers, but in effect has become a weekly meeting of Aldeanos. It begins with a short period of small-group

---

* A remarkable expression of the conflict between the priests and their parishioners was demonstrated over the music to be used at the time of communion. Dominicans are accustomed to singing a somewhat toneless recitative while filing up to the altar rail to receive the host, a form stemming from fifteenth-century Spanish liturgical music, but unknown in the United States. The organist, unable or unwilling to follow the Dominican congregation at this time, played a completely different tune at fortissimo level. The congregation and chanter sang on oblivious to the organ's competition.

meditation, and during the hour-long social period following this, individuals announce and arrange events of interest to the congregation, and give out information about the needs or illness of persons from the village. Frequently the discussion turns to events taking place in the Dominican Republic, especially as they affect Aldea or its inhabitants. Gossip gleaned from a newly arrived immigrant or visiting relative is exchanged. Occasionally visiting priests from Santiago who have at some time in the past served the congregation in Aldea are present, and answer questions about political and economic events at home. Such authoritative visitors provide valuable information and validation for the reports of less knowledgeable informants. Attempts by Padre Jesús to utilize these gatherings to give instruction in nutrition and health practices offended some, as they were interpreted as criticism of Dominican culture.

The central figure in these meetings is, of course, Padre Jesús, but he shares a leadership role with Julio, the acknowledged spokesman for Aldeano members of the congregation. However, Julio is never thought of by others as occupying a leadership role. The terms *líder, jefe,* or *presidente* would not be used as terms of reference. Rather, his right to be spokesman and counselor for the group stems from his possession of that all important trait of *confianza.* Just as most members of the school committee back in the village are judged to be *personas de confianza* because of their frequent performance of acts of charity and public service without apparent motive of personal gain, he has earned approbation for the same kind of activity. It is he more than anyone else who can be expected to call upon the sick and assist those in need, to lend small amounts of money to non-kinsmen, apparently without interest, and to attend fiestas celebrating the rites of passage of his many *compadrazgo* kinsmen. It is clear that while part of his leadership role and status emanate from linkages outside the context of the Church-supported organization, it is only within activity which has been formally sanctioned by religious authority that such leadership becomes publicly articulated. Were he neither perceived by a majority as possessing *confianza* nor supported by Padre Jesús, it is doubtful that this leadership role would emerge. The Church provides a neutral setting in which neither politics, jealousy, nor personal gain are accepted modes of behavior.

Padre Jesús periodically organizes group events for his Hispano congregation, the most popular of which are all-day Saturday trips to state park beach facilities on Long Island; the majority of the parishioners do not have automobiles and, therefore, have little access to areas not served by public transportation. Charter buses transport as many as 300 individuals, who willingly share in the cost of transportation. There is no attempt to organize group activity at these affairs; each family or friendship group remains isolated on staked-out areas of beach. There is minimal exchange or visiting between groups. Young unattached males have the most freedom to intermingle both among themselves and with the separate aggregations.

Padre Jesús has also organized dances for his Hispano congregation, but the participants are almost exclusively Dominicans. For some extended families such affairs serve as reunions, since most apartments are too small to accommodate large groups at one time.

Part of the success of Padre Jesús' activities has been his willingness to accept the role of priest as defined by the Dominicans. Their expectation includes the priest's acting as both patron and broker between themselves and "the Americans." In addition, Padre Jesús carries out his activities with few overt attempts to change their behavior; any such action is interpreted as implying criticism. "They are now asking me [it was the early part of December] to write letters to the Customs Department saying they are good, honest persons. I suppose they think they can be allowed to take in more things [on their Christmas trip to Santo Domingo]. I write such letters for them because if that is what they want, it is such a little thing to do. Perhaps it will help."

Dominican clergymen also use churches as the setting in which to appeal for funds to finance social service and charitable activities in the Republic. Padre Ricardo arrives annually, seeking money for his *Acción Social*. While in New York he preaches and celebrates mass in several churches heavily attended by his countrymen. One such trip in 1969 netted over $2,500 to buy an ambulance for the district around Aldea. Almost all this money was accumulated either through special collections taken during mass or generated from personal requests to individuals.

These institutional remittances, like the funds sent to individuals in the Republic, continue the migrants' linkage to the village. Part of the appeal for donations is based on the logic that such contributions either help one's family and friends in the village or will ultimately benefit the contributor when he returns to Santo Domingo.

In our examination of formal associational groups, we have seen how they tend at this point in time to be maladaptive in socializing (enculturating) the migrant participants to their new situation. The operation of such groups even tends to be disruptive of the development of processes which might be instrumental in the immigrant's necessary resocialization.

Secular Authorities

Another structural situation which must be noted is the very marginal membership many Dominicans have in American society, and the subsequent ease of their return to the Republic. In this situation some individuals can avoid legal sanctions that would normally be imposed on those participating fully in American society.

Usually, any possible conflict or even contact with authority figures—police, school officials, INS agents, or simply community organizers—is strictly avoided. Fear on the part of some Dominicans stems from real or imagined immigration law violations. However, for many young males, violation of the Selective Service registration regulations is the major problem. Many of those arriving in New York who are in the seventeen- to 26-year-old category do not register because they wish to avoid the possibility of being drafted. They are counseled on arrival by their more experienced New York compatriots not to register, and to take the chance that their nonregistration will go unreported. For nationalistic migrants, serving in the U.S. Army indicates that they have become Americans in the negative imperialistic sense of the word. However, for some youths from Aldea, the rationale of nonregistration is more typically built upon the premise that two years served in the Army would be two years lost to the accumulation of the capital needed to return to the Dominican Republic. While a number of Dominicans do serve in the U.S. military forces either voluntarily or after being drafted, during the entire time of my fieldwork, I was made aware of only two Aldeanos who had done so. In any case, Dominican nonregistrants reason that they can always return to Santo Domingo before the authorities have time to arrest them.

In the same manner, those individuals who become involved in crimes can readily escape prosecution by a hasty return to Santo Domingo. For example, two young male Dominicans became involved in a gun duel growing out of a dispute with a group of young Italians. A day and a half later, before the police had had an opportunity to locate and charge them, they had departed for the Dominican Republic.

This method of avoiding legal sanctions is also reported in circumstances surrounding debt collection, court ordered alimony payments, and in one case an automobile accident. Normally, such actions are accepted by other Dominicans as a justified means of escaping legal censure, and admiration is even expressed for the individual who has outwitted the Americans, especially in immigration violation cases where the law is perceived as discriminatory. The accused individual's departure is welcomed by many with whom he has maintained relations, since it allows them to escape official scrutiny. An inquiry from the police as to a person's whereabouts can then with all honesty be answered by saying he has returned to Santo Domingo. The rather tenuous ties between INS authorities and police officials result in the matter being dropped, and the individual is free to return to New York after a period of time in cases of relatively minor offenses.*

Thus some types of difficulties encountered in New York need not be resolved there, but can be avoided by escaping to the home island. Just as some individuals, who in reality reside in the Dominican Republic, retain U.S. residence visas in case of political difficulties there, the New York resident retains ties in the Dominican Republic in case of difficulties in New York.

The Travel Agent as Culture Broker **

The majority of incoming immigrants, as immediate participants in ongoing social networks, rely heavily upon the other participants as mediators between themselves and whatever aspect of the new environment they are unable to cope with. However, even the established resident Dominican is seldom so acculturated that he can provide all the assistance necessary in this highly technical and specialized U.S. society, just as native Americans at times turn to specialists in dealing with public and private bureaucracy. Because of the actual need for specialized culture broker roles and their manifestation (as *tributarios*) in the Dominican Republic, the roles are, predictably, replicated in New York. However, like almost all cultural items which undergo syncretic transformation in culture contact situations, the new role may outwardly be a familiar form in the dominant culture but given a new content under these different circumstances by bearers of the subordinate culture.

In New York, the travel agent catering to a clientele of Hispanos has undergone this process of syncretism and becomes the culture broker for large segments of Hispanic society. While such an office appears to be primarily involved in selling airline tickets and tours, it actually encompasses a host of activities which, superficially at least, seem unrelated to the travel business. A typical travel agency has

---

* These statements are based upon informant reports; police officers are reluctant to discuss this whole issue. However, one officer reported that it was not the police's job to carry out the function of INS authorities. "We'll report anyone we pick up who seems to be a visa violator, but we certainly would never go looking for them."

** Individuals who occupy roles which call for understanding of multiple cultures or subcultures and who "stand guard over crucial junctures or synapses of relations which connect" these diverse segments have been labeled culture brokers by Wolfe (1956:1075).

available translations, notary public, income tax preparation, driving instruction, real estate and rental information, foreign Spanish-language periodicals, the sale of money orders, and importantly, help in the preparation of immigrant forms. These public activities are further elaborated in more *sub rosa* services such as the extension of credit or making of small loans, sometimes at usurous rates, and highly questionable, if not illegal, participation in the recruitment of potential immigrants. Lottery tickets from the Dominican national lottery may be procured from some of these agent-brokers.* The emergence of the travel agent as such a figure is a logical development. Aside from some kind of relations with Immigration Service, the single common public activity participated in by almost all Dominicans is that dealing with travel to and from Santo Domingo. For obvious reasons legal and cultural barriers prevent representatives of the Immigration Service from emerging in these role positions as culture brokers. However, the centrality of the immigration law issue is apparent because any of the persons I would classify as a culture broker are also involved to varying degrees in the process of helping others to apply for visas. A few, notably lawyers specializing in immigration law, fall into the category of culture brokers even though they are only peripherally, if at all, involved in the selling of travel tickets.

The performance of most of these services depends upon fluency in English and familiarity with American culture forms. Much of what the enculturated American manipulates without thinking becomes formidable to the uninitiated non-English speaker. Minor items such as filling out postal change-of-address cards, alien registration forms, and securing notarized statements can take on tremendous significance, for they represent official and unintelligible documents whose importance cannot be evaluated by the migrant. Consequently, individuals perceived as experts, if only because they proclaim themselves as such, are sought out to perform these culture brokering services. Demonstrated ability to perform whatever act is bargained for is certainly an important criterion by which to judge such brokers. However, for many who desire their services, *confianza* is also essential. The potential client's residence status may be somewhat irregular, or the service desired may demand the complicity of a knowledgeable but trustworthy individual. The latter is often the case in matters centering around immigration problems. In addition, the Hispanic tradition

---

* The services rendered by the individuals listed here are not necessarily available from all of them. Some of their services are highly idiosyncratic to either the agent or to the buyer. One agent offers to transport persons to and from Kennedy Airport to greet new arrivals, at a cost triple that charged by commercial taxi. One is reminded of the cartoon character Available Jones in Al Capps' *Little Abner.* When attempting to describe the scope of their activities, his motto was "Anything available, for a price."

emphasizes the value of operating through personalitic relationships, and this results in the search for known individuals to act on one's behalf, rather than relying on impersonal formal procedures. A broker is often attributed with personal connections to influential persons. Thus a request for a visa extension is felt by many to carry more weight when filled out and handled by such a broker than if the individual were to present himself alone before immigration authorities.

Most business transactions carried out by broker-agents are lawful; some may be questionable. They are often carried out so that the broker appears to have special competence or connections, *una llave* (literally a key, that is, an official with whom he deals), and is therefore in a position to render superior service.* One informant reported to have a "friend," an agent-broker who had a special notary public seal that was recognized in public offices as being of special importance. A common practice is to accept prepayment for flights booked months in advance although the ticket is not issued until shortly before departure and hence the agent need not make payment to the airline. He thus has access to quantities of capital during this period at the expense of the client. Charges for translations are what the traffic will bear, and payments of as much as five dollars were reported for help in filling out simple one-page employment application forms. A notary seal is routinely one dollar at many such agencies "because of the translation service involved," although the same seal is available for twenty-five cents elsewhere. By the same token, some agents wave these fees for friends as an inducement to purchase other services. Normally, broker-agents steer a wide path around political affiliation and its almost inevitable bickering and divisiveness. The most successful avoid publicity, although others utilize their participation in Dominican social activities as vehicles for promoting their business activities. The editor of the Dominican page of one New York Spanish daily has organized a network of broker agencies using his well-known name as a selling point.

Not all these travel agents have offices or are authorized to issue airline tickets. Often they have arrangements with authorized issuing agencies for a split of the commission. For these brokers the focus of the relationship with their client is on the translation or broker activities and the ticket sale is an outgrowth of this, especially when they

---

* The waiting-room of one such office had walls lined with framed letters addressed to the agent from every conceivable official office including the President of the United States, governor of New York and mayor of the city. In almost all cases the letter's contents were non-committal replies thanking the agent for having written the officeholder with some suggestion or comment. However, each letter bore the official letterhead of that office and for the non-English reader, appeared to give every indication that the agent had an alarming display of powerful official connections.

have assisted an individual in applying for a visa. Helping a client find an apartment, register his child in school, or accompanying him to the police station sets up obligations to acquire tickets through him the next time that client goes to Santo Domingo.

The successful agent-broker, whether he carries on these activities as a full-time business or as a sideline, depends upon his ability to retain and form wide-ranging networks of friends and acquaintances. Even though he may become sufficiently acculturated to form social relationships with Americans and move with some ease in American society, his position requires alternating between the two cultures. Gluckman refers to this kind of behavior as "situational selection" (1958:47).

One agent-broker who has a thriving business in Upper Manhattan reflected upon his situation and expressed frustration at the duality of his role activities. "I am a Dominican, but I'm not. They are foolish to think they can go back. What would I do, open a candy store in Villalado [a settlement near Aldea]? They will always be poor *campesinos* being taken advantage of as long as they remain bound together like *guandule* [tightly compressed tobacco]. But my business and my family require that I spend much time with them. Almost any time I have free I go over to Long Island. Did you know I brought my mother up [from the Republic] last week to see a doctor?"

It would be incorrect to portray these agent-brokers as possessing an interlocking system of relationship that in effect either links themselves as a role class, or binds the majority of the immigrants together. Many Dominicans have reached the point of acculturation and literacy in English where they are either capable of acting on their own behalf or using existing American channels to accomplish their goals. However, these agent-brokers through their network of clients are able to link together far larger configurations, at least to ego-agent, than in the characteristic close-knit networks which are based exclusively on either kinship or regional relationships. In some cases, when the agent is operating informally, the client network and his familial network are by and large congruent. But even in these cases vital linkages can be traced between the authorized ticket agent and his fee-splitting subordinate. It is significant that this set of crosscutting supralocal relationships based upon socioeconomic rather than political ties has, at a minimum, incipient possibilities as a unifying force within the highly segmented Dominican and other Hispanic immigrant groups. When the police call upon one such individual to pass information into the "Dominican community" and refer to him as a "leader," they implicitly recognize the key structural position he occupies, but do not understand the basis of his so-called leadership.

CHAPTER EIGHT

Implications for the Schools

The question this study initially proposed to examine concerned the role of formal education in the acculturation process of Aldeano immigrants as participants in U.S. society. As the research progressed it became apparent that this was at most a peripheral question. Of far greater importance were the mechanisms operating to isolate them socially from extensive extra-group activities in New York. However, this isolation is not predicated upon geographical encapsulation within the confines of the city. Rather, we have seen how an extensive system of social and economic linkages to the sending society has persisted rather than attenuated over time. This has led us to view their behavior in terms of a social field of activity that includes elements in the Republic as well as New York. This is not to say that school attendance has had no impact, especially on children who have experienced formal education only in the New York context. Rather, it questions the centrality often imputed to schools in the consideration of the acculturation process. As we shall demonstrate, the schools are used selectively by parents and children to achieve valued objectives, however incongruent these objectives may be to those of the educational institution.

Rather than examine schools from the point of view of their centrality to acculturation, one might ask an alternative question: "What are the incongruencies between the cultural expectations of Aldeanos and what schools do, or what schools are perceived by them to do?" One might then speculate with reasonable certainty about some of the functional results of schools in this kind of context. Admittedly, the statements made here are from the standpoint of outsiders, including parents as well as myself, whose opportunity to view school behavior was limited. They do, however, embrace the views of important outsiders, the parents of Dominican children enrolled in the schools. I spent some time observing and interviewing school personnel, but far more outside the physical context of the school talking with parents and pupils about schools.

Before focusing specifically on Dominican pupils and parents, however, it is necessary to place these remarks in context by making some general statements about the Hispano population in relation to New York schools.

Goal Criteria of the Acculturation Process

One must first pose the question, "Acculturation to what?" New York is a cosmopolitan city. Over 20 percent of its population is of Hispano origin. This segment has been characterized as a "second city." While Hispanos are distributed throughout the city at almost all social and economic levels, major geographical, economic, and cultural concentrations may be pinpointed. They are overwhelmingly members of lower income segments. Large numbers are employed in certain occupational categories and are almost totally excluded from others. Their economic position, among other factors, relegates them to specific settlement patterns within the city and this, together with their persistent use of Spanish, serves as a significant and visible ethnic boundary to the larger society. An ethnic group-consciousness with a concomitant cultural system has emerged, an amalgam of the New World Spanish tradition with many North American borrowings. This Hispano subculture or subsociety has developed a cultural pattern that is a yet uncompleted synthesis symbiotic to New York.

More and more public schools are coming to reflect this new state of stabilized cultural pluralism. In many schools over half the students are Spanish-speaking ethnics. For most of these children attendance represents an opportunity to acquire biculturalism in the sense Polgar uses the term: "concurrent socialization into two or more cultures whenever a situation of stabilized pluralism obtains" (1960:217). But in schools with large enrollments of children who identify themselves as Hispanos, the second culture is often likely to be the cultural equivalent of "Spanglish," rather than the dominant American culture.

Ethnic Demography of the Public Schools

Contemporary changes in the ethnic composition of New York City's general population are reflected in similar shifts in the characteristics of the public school-attending population.* During the 1960's

---

* Because of the skewed demographic characteristics of the City's population, school enrollments do not mirror the general population distribution since large segments are single or in stages of their life cycle that preclude them from having any school-age children. In addition, large numbers of middle- and upper-class children are enrolled in other than public schools and, therefore, are not included in these public school enrollment statistics.

Puerto Rican pupils jumped from 16.1 percent to 22.8 percent of the total register, while blacks increased from 22.8 percent to 34.4 percent; the "others" category declined from 61.1 percent to 42.8 percent. It was not until 1968 that annual school censuses attempted to identify non-Puerto Rican children of Hispanic origin as a separate category; previously if they were known not to be Puerto Rican they were all placed in the "other" category.* The figures suggest the differential territorial settlement patterns between Puerto Ricans and "other Hispanos," especially when a district-by-district comparison is made. In the Bronx, for example, 42.8 percent of the elementary school register are Puerto Rican but only 2.5 percent "other Hispanos." In Manhattan 34.4 percent are Puerto Rican but 8.6 percent are "other Spanish surnamed Americans." In District #6 (the Upper West Side of Manhattan), there are fewer Puerto Ricans than "others" (17.6 percent vs. 33.2 percent). In five districts in Queens, the "other Spanish" outnumber the Puerto Ricans.

If the total population of Spanish-speaking New York ethnics is divided about equally between Puerto Ricans and "other Spanish," the question arises as to why this distribution is not evidenced in school enrollment figures. Several of the many reasons for this are particularly relevant within the Dominican context. First, the recency of the migration and the age of the migrants have not yet allowed for the formation of marital unions whose temporal developmental cycle would have produced many school-aged children. Secondly, the very nature of the immigration is one in which large numbers of children are left behind, or in some cases sent back to the Republic for schooling. In addition, one might suggest that the figures are erroneous in that the enumerators lacked the information to distinguish between Puerto Ricans and "others," especially in upper grades where the relationships between teacher and student are usually tenuous and impersonal.

While it is my impression that relatively few marital unions take place between Puerto Ricans and other nationalities within the Spanish-speaking population of New York City, when they do, the resulting

---

* The accuracy of these counts is to be questioned on another basis, too. "When these data were collected, the schools were instructed to obtain the count of children . . . by inspection only. In other words, pupils were not questioned about their respective ethnic backgrounds. The final determination of the category in which each child belonged was made at the local level [Board of Education, 1970:1]." Based upon my interviews with classroom teachers, who were ultimately responsible for making these counts, but who often had limited knowledge of the backgrounds of their pupils, I question how accurate and even how conscientiously the census was made. The census posed many problems, one of them being, what constitutes a "Spanish surname"? A glance at the telephone book of any Latin American city reveals how many non-Spanish surnames can be found in these countries.

children are counted as Puerto Rican. This method of categorization tends to give Puerto Ricans a higher representation than if the nationality of the other parent were counted.

PRESENT FOCUS ON PUERTO RICANS

A vast bibliography documents various aspects of the influx of Puerto Ricans into the New York school systems (Cordasco 1967, 1968). Some studies and accounts examine both the psychological and sociological effects this growth and in-migration have had upon individuals and institutions. Others scrutinize curricular content and pedagogical techniques best suited to meet the needs of this burgeoning population. However, little cognizance has been paid of the growing non-Puerto Rican Hispanic population in this body of literature. The reasons for this are somewhat similar to those for the relative ignorance of the authorities regarding the demographic characteristics of population: the recency of migration, the tendency of the wider society to categorize all Spanish speakers as Puerto Ricans, the political expediency of failing to recognize their existence, and the impact that legal and ecologic factors have upon migration. Certainly it is important that, since they make up only 3.4 percent of the total public school population, they are placed far down the list of priorities in the extensive catalogue of problems plaguing the system. Among school personnel and others there is an implicit assumption that a pan-Hispanic cultural tradition exists, allowing for very little national deviation or specialization.

The majority of Spanish-speaking personnel in the New York schools is Puerto Rican; they generally are in roles such as community liaison workers or teacher's aides. They occupy pivotal roles in interpreting the Spanish-speaking community to English-speaking school personnel. In interviews and observations of both types of personnel an unawareness of the degree of national cleavages that exists among the Hispano population is apparent. There is a real possibility of unconscious distortion in the interpretation of one Hispanic group by another.

Mrs. Nuñez, an educated articulate Puerto Rican, came to New York seventeen years ago when she was 20. She is a community relations worker in an area with a high concentration of Dominicans and other Hispanos, but relatively few Puerto Ricans. In an interview, she characterized Dominicans as "much lower class than Puerto Ricans. They live and act like animals. They are what we call *brutos*. . . . The Cubans are snobs; they think they have more rights as refugees than Puerto Ricans. The United States should take care of its own people first." She was praised by the school principal as a community leader on whom "we must rely heavily . . . to tell us what is going on with our parents and our community."

This is not to deny that it is possible to isolate among Hispanic peoples a configuration of values that represent a "culture focus" loosely identifiable within their own self-identification as members of *La Raza.* What needs to be clarified is that at this point in time neither is it accurate to allow one subset to be identified as representative model of the whole, nor is it justifiable to allow one group to act as spokesman for the whole. Any observer armed with a modicum of information about the New York Hispano population begins to see the configuration of cleavages based up on both political-national and socioeconomic constructs. One of the present problems is that uninformed political decisions based upon uncritical assumptions have led to biases about the nature of the Spanish-speaking population, its desires and needs.

What follows are observations about one such subgroup and its relationship to schools. In many ways its reaction is quite similar to that of other Hispanos; indeed, its criticism and discontent often coincide with those of a very broad spectrum of New York residents, cutting across class, economic, and ethnic lines.

Value Perspective of the School

It is part of the role of a proper Dominican parent to send his children to school. As has been pointed out, in the Republic one of the parameters involved in social valuation is educational attainment. The mere act of coming to New York enhances the individual's status in the eyes of those within his social field. Therefore, it is not unexpected that New York immigrants, especially those whose presence is more than temporary, regardless of their long-term commitment, place strong emphasis on school attendance for their children who are too young to work.

Education is prized almost universally for its instrumental value by Aldeano parents in New York. But the components of this instrumental value vary from individual to individual. For most, schooling is seen as a means for learning English and hence, greater control of their destiny in New York, since employment range and resulting economic opportunities are greatly expanded for those who can use English effectively. However, for some this positive valuation can be withdrawn whenever it is perceived that school attendance no longer has such a functional value. When a teenager reaches a level of language competence whereby he can obtain a "good" job or, in rare cases, where a "good" job is found which is not dependent upon language, parental support for school attendance is often withheld. This is especially the case where no ideological commitment to remaining in New York has been made.

For other parents the formal education of their children represents public and private validation of the geographical move from the *campo* to New York, as well as the social transition from *campesino* to—at least—proletarian New Yorker. For this group, Greer's argument that the New York schools have served far less as a route to social mobility than as a validation of this mobility would seem pertinent.

Public education was the rubber stamp of economic improvement, rarely has it been the bootstrap . . . : the key factor is more probably the indigenous grounding of the unit within the ethnic boundary—the establishment of an ethnic middle class before scaling the walls of the dominant society (1969:11).

But the lack of any diachronic view of this process requires that it remain only a hypothesis in relation to Aldeanos. Since only a handful of their children have attended New York schools for any length of time, it is difficult to make any judgments or give evidence on any patterning of behavior. At this point, however, the criterion for success from the parental viewpoint is still drawn from their own Dominican experience, not from dominant American attitudes toward education. I encountered only two Aldeano parents who even contemplated the possibility of post-secondary-school education for their children. For the majority, support for school attendance is rapidly withdrawn after the child reaches employable age, or, in the case of girls, is eligible for marriage. Nevertheless, parents almost invariably include the importance of the opportunity for schooling for their children when they recite reasons for migrating to New York, though this ranks below economic reasons.

The value placed on schooling is visible in many living rooms where framed school certificates, graduating diplomas from elementary or secondary schools, and even the official-appearing certificate of completion of a correspondence course, are prominently hung on the walls. For some families school graduations call for a public demonstration in the form of a family *fiesta*, or more simply, a family outing to the beach or to *una feria*, Coney Island, for example.

Elena, the nineteen-year-old eldest daughter and second of eight children, graduated from a public high school after spending ten of her school years in New York schools. She was the first person to do so among her father's extended family of ten siblings, all of whom presently live in New York. The occasion called for a fiesta at which members of the families of six of her uncles and aunts were present. During the course of the party her uncle José, the most eloquent of the group, read a two-page speech he had spent long hours preparing extolling the honor she had brought to the entire family's name through graduation. At the same time he reiterated the need to hold fast to the beautiful *cultura Dominicana*.

Certainly for many parents an additional motivation for sending children to school is that it leaves adults free to seek employment by relieving them of child-care responsibilities. Especially in some of the crowded areas of Manhattan, school is considered the safest place for children, other than the home and the church. Otherwise they are largely kept within the confines of the household. To allow them to be on the streets without supervision is considered dangerous because of traffic and the possibility of contact with drug addicts and other undesirable persons. Many conscientious parents fear that unsupervised play will allow their children to learn such "American" habits as disrespect for adults.

Patterns of School Attendance

It is difficult to make more than broad generalizations about patterns of school attendance among Aldeano immigrant children. Most of those under sixteen are enrolled in and attend some school, if for no other reason than that they are legally required to do so.

A successful learning experience which results in the willingness of the pupil to remain in school is often related to the age at which English-language schooling begins. Younger children experience far less difficulty than older ones as a result of both the content and methodology of the elementary school curriculum. Elementary teachers, for example, have far fewer assumptions about the level of academic competence of pupils than secondary teachers necessarily do. As a result, the mutual expectations of both teacher and pupil are more compatible at elementary than higher levels. Thus pupils who start in the New York school system at an earlier age experience less difficulty with language and cultural problems than those who migrate north at a later age, and they persist in attending school for a longer time.

When a choice is possible, parents often deem it most convenient to leave children already in their early adolescence in the village until they are old enough to work. Their concern is not that a New York school will not provide an education but that a person of this age who is neither attending school nor working has no social role. He is a potential *tigre* (juvenile delinquent), and thus a possible source of trouble with the police and other authorities, a prospect understandably avoided by persons who perceive their status even as legal immigrants to be somewhat precarious.

In comparison with other Dominican youths from urban backgrounds, very few Aldeanos have had secondary school experience in New York. Eight of the eleven high school students on whom data are available are female. For the most part, those attending school seldom achieved grade placement above the intermediate-junior high school levels. This relatively low achievement level results from a combination of factors: limited previous school experience in the Republic, the age at which the migration took place, and parental support for continuing in school vis-à-vis seeking employment. Early marriage was a reason for several girls discontinuing school, although at least one completed high school while living with a young Aldeano male.

Apparent throughout discussions about schooling is the continuity between patterns of school attendance in the village and in New York. Parents who express interest or concern about schooling in New York are almost without exception those who have, by village standards, considerable school experience themselves, and are often from families where schooling is a general concern. At the fiesta celebrating Elena's graduation, I remembered her grandmother's home in the village, where one end of the living room was equipped like a school room, with a school bench and a small blackboard, on which conjugated forms of an English verb were written.

Parental Nonparticipation in School Activities

School personnel often commented on the difficulty they had in getting Dominican parents to participate in any sort of parent-school relationship. "They are too busy making money to take part," was a consistent and somewhat sarcastic characterization of Dominicans by primarily Puerto Rican Spanish-speaking staff members. Such a statement has a grain of partial truth in it, but one must remember that even those immigrants who make long-term commitments to New York are starting from scratch in terms of material possessions and are usually burdened by social and financial obligations incurred in the process of entering the U.S. Parents who work at manual tasks during the day are seldom enthusiastic about encounters with unknown situations in the evening, and to visit a school during the day when teachers are present often means a financial loss.

But economic factors are only part of the reason for nonparticipation. A number of others may be noted, their saliency varying from individual to individual. The ethic of nonparticipation which arises from deep-rooted sociohistorical factors in the Republic, in addition to the presence of illegal residents within the New York colony, inhibits open participation or affiliation with any public grouping. Certainly for some, intra- and interethnic group competition is important, and participation often entails interacting and cooperating with *los negros* (the black ones). The desire to remain socially distant from American

Negroes stems from both a physical fear and the desire not to be categorized with them. The school and its personnel represent for some an encapsulation of their relationship to the dominant culture—fear of its superiority and impersonality ("I don't go to school because I don't want to be lectured"), an assumption of their own inadequacy compared to those *inteligente* (intelligent and clever) Americans. Yet some have a sense, bordering on contempt, that the Americans can never master or match the spirit embodied in *La Raza*. "They don't and they can't understand us, we're uncomfortable with Americans."

My research was begun during a prolonged teachers' strike in the city of New York. Attempts to open the schools or hold classes in facilities other than school buildings were made in many districts. For the most part, parents had little knowledge of the issues and were reluctant to get involved. Since most often they had to rely on their children for information concerning the availability of classes and teachers, it would seem that pupil attendance depended upon what information each child decided to give his parents. The most common complaint on the part of parents was the disruption caused in their lives when schools could not perform their normal custodial function.

CONFLICTING VALUES OF TEACHER ROLE BEHAVIOR

Dominican parents have serious reservations about New York schools, especially public ones, when the schools' practices are contrary to their values. For example, an Aldeano typically views the school and its teachers as extensions of the family. The ascribed role of a teacher in many respects parallels that of the Dominican father: stern, autocratic, demanding, deserving unquestioned deference. A real conflict develops for Dominican parents as well as pupils when the New York teacher fails to meet these role expectations. For most North Americans the ideal behavior of a teacher indicates a student-teacher relationship of helpfulness and collegiality with muted expression of subordinate-superordinate distinctions. This collegiality is perceived as signs of weakness, incompetence, or even effeminateness by Dominicans, who interpret North American pedagogical techniques aimed at eliciting reasoned responses rather than rote memorization as nonteaching. This same process, to whatever degree it is successful, ultimately leads the student to question authority and is in direct conflict with idealized behavioral patterns in Dominican culture.

I accompanied a Dominican parent to school to talk with his child's teacher about the boy's disciplinary problems in school, and we were invited to view an experimental classroom which it was thought might be helpful in solving the youngster's problem. All the classroom's traditional furniture had been removed and was replaced by a number of low tables. Half the room was furnished with well-worn carpeting and overstuffed chairs where the children could retire when they became disinterested in projects that were presented by their teachers. The three adults assigned to the classroom interacted with the children on a highly individual basis with a great deal of individual physical contact taking place between teachers and pupils. While we were in the room a bearded young male teacher, dressed in corduroy trousers and open-collared denim shirt, came into the room and greeted the pupils with a friendly wave and then bussed one of the females on the cheek. The parent was horrified by the scene of what he considered chaos and inappropriate role behavior. For him, whatever it was that was taking place in the room was not learning and he wanted no part of it for his child. This experimental unit was later abandoned, not because of its lack of success in dealing with children who had behavioral and learning problems in a traditional setting, but rather because of parental protest over the non-traditional approach to learning.

Dominican child-training practices are based on the idea that very young children are incapable of making rational decisions and therefore should not be expected to meet very exacting standards. This attitude was forcefully brought out in another context in the Dominican Republic where I observed child-training practices of Dominicans vis-à-vis British West Indians. Each group was critical of the other because of the level of expectations or lack thereof for the upbringing of their offspring. "He's too young to understand," says the Dominican. "He must be trained and then he know," retorted the West Indian neighbor.

At the age of six or seven, acceptable behavior patterns change radically. Within a short period of time, the child is expected to conform to adult-like behavior. Surrounded as he is by family and kinsmen, he is vulnerable to considerable social pressure short of physical punishment. Except for one occasion when a father was drunk, I witnessed no scenes of physical punishment and only a few of loud or sharp reprimand. When a teacher in a New York classroom, for whatever reason, loses his temper and reprimands a pupil loudly or sarcastically, the Dominican pupils, especially older males, are threatened by what appears to them to be overresponsive behavior and a loss of teacher dignity.

Return Migration for Schooling

The perceived transitory nature of most immigrants' stay in New York has other repercussions in relation to the school. Just as upper-class Dominicans send their children abroad to study, especially to the United States, Spain, and Mexico, so some New York residents have sought to return their children to the Republic for schooling.

Reasons for doing so range from the inability of the children to adjust to U.S. schools to parents' fear that their children will be acculturated as Americans. Certainly many of those sending their children back to private schools in the Republic would have been unable to do so for financial and social reasons had they themselves not migrated; this is especially true of former *campesinos*. Such actions, even if undertaken by only a small minority of New York residents, illustrate upward mobility within the framework of the immigrants' social field. Just as individuals who for one reason or another come into conflict with U.S. authorities can quietly slip back to the Republic, so can pupils who for whatever reason fail to adjust to the school situation in New York return to their homeland for schooling there. In the village school at the time of my research, only one pupil was enrolled who had formerly attended school in New York, but a number of cases were cited in which parents from the village had returned their children to the Republic to attend urban boarding schools. This, however, is much more typical of former urbanites than *campesinos*.

Julio, fifteen, born in Aldea, had lived for several years in Upper Manhattan with his divorced mother. He had had disciplinary difficulties in the sixth grade which his mother blamed upon his difficulties in learning English. She arranged for him to return to La Vega where his fraternal grandparents lived and enrolled him in a *colegio*. I met him while interviewing his mother during the summer of 1969, when he had returned to New York for a visit with her. His two-year experience in the *colegio* had left him politically radicalized and he was critical of New York schools because they failed to participate in politicalization of their pupils. For him at least, the result of his mother's migration to New York was to socialize the progeny of a *campesino* into a middle-class Dominican youth.

Parochial Schools

Since both in popular belief and in fact privately operated schools in the Dominican Republic are physically and educationally better than public schools, it is natural that New York residents consider parochial schools better than public ones. This is not a valuation unique to Dominicans; private and parochial schools educate a large portion of the pupil population of New York City. Aldeano parents unanimously expressed a desire to me that their children should attend Church-supported schools.* However, many could not send their

* As has been noted, Aldeanos are concentrated in two areas of New York City and great numbers of them attend the parish churches in these respective areas. The comments here are based upon interviews and observations made in the parish schools as well as more general interviews and readings about parochial educational problems in the City.

children to such schools because of the expense involved, their lack of availability in the neighborhood, or inability of the schools to deal with large numbers of non-English speakers. All Aldeano parochial school enrollees reported were on the elementary level.

As well as assuming the academic superiority of parochial schools, parents also reason that these schools by the nature of their operation are more in accord with the behaviors they value. "In the public schools they learn to be disrespectful of parents and older people. . . . The school in the church doesn't allow them to disobey and do all the things like fighting and using drugs like the public school does." These were typical explanations of why parents preferred their children to attend a parochial school, even though the small tuition payments represented considerable drain on the family's economic resources. But Church-supported schools are under considerable economic strain themselves, and parish resources are hard put to keep them in operation. As a result, the service these schools offer varies. Even when those responsible for the operation of the parochial school are ideologically committed to helping immigrant children attend their schools, the language problem is considerable. "We simply don't have the money and the teachers for teaching in two languages. They must go to the public schools to learn enough English so that we can work with them. The public schools have the machines and the teachers for such things," said the priest in one lower East Side parish; he was working hard to help his Dominican parishioners. One nun-teacher of this parish was sent to a convent in Spain to learn Spanish in order to work with these pupils. The other school, located in Queens, expressed a similar attitude about the need for pupils to be able to express themselves in English before enrolling, but for different reasons. The administration considered English the language in which teachers should teach and pupils must learn. Public schools in these two areas all have some form of extensive bilingual programs available.

It might be noted that five girls originally from Aldea have been sent to a convent boarding school in Vermont. Four of them have been withdrawn either because they disliked it or because in 1969 there was a drastic upward shift in the cost of matriculating there, and parents felt they could no longer afford it.

In the Schools

ENTRY PROBLEMS: GRADE PLACEMENT

Given the rate of retention of pupils in lower grades in Aldea, it is quite possible that when a ten-year-old arrives in New York, he may have achieved only the first level, either repeating it several times or dropping out of school altogether. Even so, he would normally be enrolled in a New York school, if for no other reason than its custodial functions. One of the difficulties faced by any school which must deal with transient populations is the placement of new enrollees. Within the North American system this is partially resolved through a system of records and transcripts transmitted from school to school. But this system of record-keeping is all but unknown in the Republic and so the individual (usually a counselor) charged with placement must make immediate decisions based upon almost no information. Compounding this problem is the fact that the counselor seldom speaks Spanish and consequently, must rely upon either some Spanish-speaking individual from within the school system or someone who accompanies the enrollee to act as translator-broker.

This problem of assignment to a specific classroom, teacher, or grade is compounded by the inability to translate grade levels from one cultural context to another. Even if it were possible to draw some relationship between *curso II* and second grade, the high retention rate in the Republic makes it not unusual for a twelve-year-old to present himself as a first- or second-grader. The New York City school system, like most of the American educational establishment, assumes in both regulation and practice that there is no great discontinuity between the psychophysical developmental levels of members of a grade level. The characterization of a gangly adolescent who has failed repeatedly and is crowded at a first-grader's desk is held up for derision and interpreted as an indictment of the school rather than of the child. Thus, the entering twelve-year-old is placed in fifth or sixth grade regardless of his placement in the Republic. This situation is often used by both the Dominican parent and students and American educators as a basis for deriding the educational process and institutions of the other society. For the Dominican the placement of a child in a higher class only reinforces the low esteem held for American schools, because it demonstrates that one does learn more in schools at home, while the American educators express condescension toward backward, old-fashioned schools that are not concerned about the psychosocial needs of the pupils.

Another example of the lack of articulation between schools is the frequent complaint by New York school personnel that they can elicit no response from Dominican schools when they request forwarding of school records. Explanations that the schools seldom keep such records and even if they did would have no postage available to send it, usually reinforce the low opinion of these schools.

SPECIAL PROGRAMS: SOCIALIZATION FOR SEPARATISM

But this arbitrary assignment of the incoming pupil to a grade is purely an administrative categorization. All the public schools I visited had some form of special instruction for the non-English-speaking student. Such programs vary from school to school and a variety of nomenclature is used to denote the special ideology or methodology assumed to underlie the individual programs. Regardless of the theoretical assumptions rationalizing these programs, all are equivocated by the availability of resources and personnel to carry the program out.

One such program was built around the idea of close articulation between home, community, and school, but for the first six months of the school year it had no Spanish-speaking liaison between the community and the school, though some 60 percent of its population was Hispanic. A bureaucratic regulation concerning teacher space allocations prevented the assignments of such a person, although it was recognized by all that this was a key position in the pilot program. Another program places the new student in a regular classroom, but he is segregated for as much as half of each day in some form of remedial instruction primarily focused on language acquisition. Such segregation poses problems of internal and external identification as a deviate group similar to those encountered when ability grouping is practiced within a school. Some schools aim at bilingual instruction in which regular academic subjects are taught in Spanish, and English is learned as a functional second language.

Even if resources are available, one important element hindering the development of such programs is the general lack of agreement about the school's role in the acculturation and socialization of its Spanish-speaking clientele. This in turn is a reflection of American societal indecision about acceptance of either the ideology or reality of social and cultural pluralism. Within a given school one finds teachers who actively promote the retention of Spanish language and cultural patterns even at the price of promoting social segregation. Others, usually older teachers, oppose with equal strength but less vociferously any change in the school system that indicates the school is not, as common belief would have it, the essential institution in acculturating the foreigner to the dominant culture. It is doubtful that the ultimate determination of the school's role in this crucial social decision will be made by the educational establishment itself; rather it will be played out in a much wider framework within the developmental history of ethnicity in the United States.

Institutionalized segregation in the form of special language classes, remedial classes, tracking, or bilingual education, as well as the more subtle forms of segregation emanating from a variety of assumptions within the dominant society about Hispanos, coupled with activities of self-segregation, all combine to socialize many pupils into a heightened consciousness, however inarticulate, of a distinct ethnic identity—either as Dominicans or Hispanos. A study of Haitian pupils in New York schools concluded that schools, along with other public institutions, in attempting to provide recognition of the cultural diversity of their clientele, inadvertently create an "organizational vessel" (see Barth 1969:14) in which opportunity is given to express ethnic identity (Nina Glick, personal communication). The search by political units, for example, for Haitian or Dominican representatives to speak for their respective "community," is one form of this assistance in the creation of what might otherwise remain a latent or unexpressed ethnicity. The schools, by competing for limited available resources to create special programs catering to and identifying with specific ethnic sets or subsets, have been instrumental in the coalescence and articulation of this identity. Indeed, the schools—and the battles over decentralization that have raged through the system during the past decade—have provided one of the few political areas in which black and Hispano ethnic minorities have been able to gain control (cf Hendricks 1973, and Vincent 1970). However, at this time Aldean parents and their student offspring are not directly participating in this social process, although they obviously cannot remain unaffected by it.

PARENTAL REACTION TO SPECIAL PROGRAMS

Parental attitudes about such programs as those aimed at reinforcing Spanish language and Hispanic culture are far from uniform. In a general way one can categorize responses to questions concerning the value of such programs along a continuum representing the individual's attitude toward the functional value of school attendance itself. Those who see school as the place for learning English and skills for coping with the dominant culture are less supportive of such programs than are parents and students who are more reluctant to lose their social and nationalistic identity as either Dominicans or Hispanos. Most Aldeanos fall into the first category and the immigrants from the urban politicized intellectual classes into the latter. The few Dominicans who have spoken out publicly have been drawn from the urbanized, extremely nationalistic segment of the immigrant population. School authorities would be badly misled to assume that these individuals express an opinion arrived at through any accord. Although few *campesinos* can articulate their feelings as neatly, the consensus of this group would be that they prefer a program allowing their children to retain what they feel to be their unique national and cultural identity, but not at the expense of not acquiring those tools of the dominant culture that are thought to be instrumental in competing for economic and even social equality. "In my house we speak Spanish. I can teach my children about my country. I cannot speak good English and my wife knows none. That is why I send them to school. No, I don't want them to forget they are Dominicans, but we live in New York," said a 35-year-old father of three.

SEEKING A STANDARD SPANISH

Even under the best of circumstances an issue which seldom surfaces at the official level is that of deciding what constitutes a standard form of Spanish to be taught. The Hispano is usually amused and often openly critical when the American teacher tries to pronounce and speak Spanish as a second language, and some characterize it as *macarrónico* (pig-Latin) (*El Tiempo,* November 17, 1970). There are in fact distinct national, regional, and class variants of pronunciation and nomenclature. Many Spanish-speaking individuals are now third- and even fourth-generation immigrants, and a distinct language drift has taken place as their speech incorporates terminology and forms from New York English. *Factoría* (factory) is substituted for *fábrica, norsa* (nurse) for *enfermera,* and one mops the floor with a *mapo* rather than a *trapeador.** Nationalistic pride and intragroup competition are exhibited in the language issue. Spanish-language radio stations must carefully balance their announcing staffs in order to avoid the criticism that one group is overrepresented.

New York schools welcomed the Cuban refugees, many of whom were former teachers and met formal U.S. teacher certification requirements in terms of university preparation, experience, and ability to speak English. However, other Hispanic groups criticized this "Cubanization" of the schools. The director of Spanish-language programs in the schools of one diocese, himself a Puerto Rican, expressed concern that as a result of the over-abundance of Cuban teachers in his system, "My people will forget their speech."

* The New York street version of Spanish has been called Spanglish. An attempt by the New School to offer a course in Spanglish aimed at helping those individuals such as social workers and teachers who of necessity must communicate with the clients on a street speech level led to violent protests in the Spanish press as a "murder attempt . . . of the most beautiful language in the world. . . ."; also "Anglo-Saxon concept of the inferiority of the Puerto Rican people." "The permanent alienation from both North America and Latin America" (*The New York Times,* December 28, 1970:33).

ADULT FORMAL INSTRUCTIONAL ACTIVITIES

In addition to educational facilities for preadolescents and adolescents, there are numerous post-school opportunities in New York for adults to learn English or acquire specific occupational skills. Although the majority of adult Aldeanos never participate in these—only seven percent on whom data was available indicated they had—enough have done so to allow speculation as to why most have not. As might be anticipated, there is a close correlation between previous education and the willingness to participate and ability to succeed in most of these situations. Additional factors include the individual's legal status and his social and economic obligations.

Two individuals in their late 30's who had lived in New York for relatively lengthy periods (six and eight years) were both proud to display their eighth-grade equivalency certificates which they had earned by attending night classes in a nearby public school. José had completed his second year of secondary school in the Republic and had been a rural elementary teacher prior to his immigration. He started night school one year after arriving in New York, having decided that without English he was doomed to remain an unskilled clothing factory worker. At the time of his night school attendance he also went to barber school and opened a small shop catering primarily to Dominicans from the Cibao. He and his wife are childless and she works as a machine operator and still speaks no English. Andreas had studied several years in a *colegio* in preseminary training. After a long day at his factory job he was tired, and his responsibilities to his growing brood of children left little time for attendance at night school. Although he eventually completed the eighth-grade class, it was reported to be at great physical and psychological cost. Even after achieving this goal of eighth-grade equivalency, neither José nor Andreas spoke English well enough to be employed in English-language situations. They did, however, serve in broker roles for those who had no competency at all in English.

It is usually younger single adults with considerable school experience who are willing and able to attempt any formalized educational experiences. However, given the degree of literacy of the typical immigrant from Aldea, the very nature of the selection process for participation in such training tends to be exclusive. During the time of my research Federal money was available under the Manpower Training Act for training the unskilled and unemployed. Among the programs available in some New York centers were those offering intensive English language instruction plus skill training. The participants were given grants of more than $50 a week for six months to a year to take this training. Unfortunately, the language-training programs, even though based upon aural-oral teaching techniques and led by dedicated knowledgeable teachers, assumed a minimal literacy in some language and effectively screened out most of those for whom the program had been requested. One such class with a 60 percent Dominican membership was made up entirely of secondary school graduates. The regulations of another class required that the men wear coats and ties. The rationale for this was, "They must become accustomed to real job situations."

Commercially operated training schools and classes are normally given in English and assume the participants to have at least a functional knowledge of the language. Thus, breaking into this cycle is not easy. The most important factor in keeping Aldeanos from engaging in such activities is that they often require a delay in getting jobs. There are great pressures to remain gainfully employed, and the newcomer rarely arrives with any extra money which would allow him to remain jobless. Those who migrate for the express purpose of accumulating capital are seldom willing to put off their earning activities.

For many, previous academic experience has not been successful and school, even attending the city-sponsored class on oil burner operation required for licensing as a building superintendent, is a threatening experience. Older men perceive such instruction as something denigrating to their age-grade male role. Immigration status may be an important factor. One intensive English class offered free by a social service-minded group of Catholics ran into difficulty at the first session when the teacher asked for participants' names and addresses. Two individuals withdrew rather than give this information, and one other gave a false address. It was determined later that the two were present in New York on expired visitors' visas and the third had acquired his visa illegally in the Republic.

CHAPTER NINE

Conclusion

This study of a group of peasants from a rural village in the Dominican Republic who have settled in New York City has described the social processes triggered by both the process of their immigration and the resultant resocialization as they adapt to their new social and cultural environment. It has shown that the important variables influencing the direction of these social processes includes the nature of the cultural experience in the sending society, the legal and social mechanisms involved in the process of entering the United States, and the socioeconomic niche they have come to occupy in the receiving society of New York. Changes in technology, especially in both modes of transportation and methods of communication, because they allow for the retention of traditional social ties, make an understanding of the sending society essential to any attempt to explain immigrant behavior.

A further social structural element of great import is that the group here described is part of a larger emergent group that for lack of a better term might be called a Spanglish subculture in New York. The process of syncretism of cultural and social elements drawn from a variety of Hispano- and Anglo-American experiences from which Spanglish emerged is far from complete. I have drawn upon the concept of retribalization to describe the constituents of this process because that concept emphasizes the retention of essential elements of the world view into which the immigrant has been acculturated while acknowledging that fundamental changes take place in the content of his experiences as a result of immigration and resettlement. Part of this is bound up in the nature of the commitment to permanent resettlement that the individual brings with him to New York. In addition I was able to delineate a developmental sequence, together with its component elements, through which the immigrant passes as he is enculturated into Spanglish society.

While this particular Dominican population is but a minute segment of the total Spanish-speaking population of New York City, it is a reasonable assumption that the problems confronting them and the mechanisms of adaptation they use are not unique to them. It is my belief that they might be considered prototypical of a fairly sizeable number of the current in-migrating Spanish-speaking population of New York City, especially of other non-Puerto Rican Spanish-speaking peasants and proletariat who began the migration process later than did Puerto Ricans.

The focus on the role of the school and its interaction with this group is admittedly partly a result of my own biases. But I believe that a solid case can be made for such an approach for several reasons. Because of the size and ubiquitousness of the educational establishment, the school is the single public institution, except perhaps for the Immigration and Naturalization Service, with whom the majority of our immigrants are forced in some fashion to deal. The school is generally imputed, correctly or not, to have been effective in the past as the acculturating agent for new immigrant populations. A detailed examination of one public agency and its interaction with the target population should suggest to the reader how one might extrapolate the relationship to other agencies. For example, both the nature of the commitment to stay in New York and the individual's assumed tenuous legal status are shown to be important factors in explaining the nature of the relationship that develops between the school and its Dominican clientele. These same factors are instrumental in partially explaining behavior toward most other institutions and agencies who attempt to deal with them.

As a major and visible social institution schools cannot help but reflect in their operation, organization, and structure the stresses and strains of the dynamic society of which they are part. They cannot remain aloof from the kind of information presented in this book if they are to deal effectively with their clientele. The whole issue of developing ethnic segmentation and resultant social pluralism may well be played out in the schools, but it cannot be assumed that educational professionals are to be left by default as the ultimate social decision-maker. As I have shown, the dilemma of this new immigrant population not only includes problems faced by almost all previous incoming groups, but also the conflicts inherent in times of radical social change. It is my belief that the information and conceptualizations generated out of such micro-studies as this of one of the multitude of populations within the modern city are essential if we are to make the necessary intelligent, educated, and rational social decisions.

Appendices

Appendix A

Population Estimates

To place the Dominican migration in context, it is necessary to examine available demographic data and speculate about the size of this population and those of its characteristics which are important to this study.

PROBLEMS OF DETERMINING HISPANO POPULATION SIZE

Ascertaining the size of the non-Puerto Rican Spanish-speaking population of New York is extremely difficult. This is a result of a number of factors: the recency of immigration, a conscious effort on the part of many of the immigrants to maintain a nonidentity, and political and institutional indifference to their numbers.

The large-scale immigration of these people has been a phenomenon of the past decade and therefore, the group was barely visible in the data generated by the 1960 U.S. census. Subsequent population estimates based upon this data perpetuate this lack of record. It has been shown that past censuses failed to record large numbers of lower-class individuals in urban areas (Pritzher 1967). While this particular failure in the collection of census data has been most often demonstrated when the urban black population is under discussion, the bulk of the Spanish-speaking population is in the same category and is under-represented for the same reasons. An effort was made in 1970 by Puerto Rican organizations to get this constituency counted when they assisted the Census Bureau in the enumeration of heavily populated Spanish-speaking areas. However, the final estimate of 1,150,000 New York City residents whose mother tongue is Spanish has been seriously questioned (Bureau of Census 1972).

Alien Address Reports, are frequently cited when demographic statements are made about nonnative Americans residing in New York. These Reports are derived from the annual registration required of all aliens residing in the U.S. However, anyone working with alien groups in New York City is well aware of how many individuals fail to register through indifference, ignorance, or wish to remain unidentified. Consequently, these reports from the INS give a depressed figure.

Methods by which demographic information is reported have also operated to conceal the national distributions within the Spanish-speaking population. Until very recently, few statistical tables concerning foreign populations in the United States attempted to distinguish those from the Dominican Republic as a separate category, but lumped them together with other groups under some rubric such as "other Caribbean" or "other Latin American." The New York public school and Catholic parochial school systems have only recently begun to make the distinction between "Puerto Ricans" and "other Spanish surnames" in their ethnic censuses.

A further factor which serves to mask the identification of non-Puerto Rican Hispanic groups is that since the city has contained large numbers of Puerto Ricans for several decades, it is fairly easy for any native Spanish speaker to either pose or allow himself to be identified as a Puerto Rican. Certainly other Spanish speakers can identify them as non-Puerto Rican but few persons in authority have the linguistic background to do so. By the same token, there is a tendency on the part of the non-Hispanic society to categorize and stereotype all Spanish speakers as Puerto Ricans. While there is a vague recognition on the part of political bodies such as city governmental agencies of the presence of subsections within the larger Hispanic group, no particular concern is evidenced for their special consideration since they are seldom citizens and do not represent any electorate. On the other hand, Puerto Rican leaders have much to gain by conspiring in this silence; they gain the political leverage that emanates from the sheer visible numbers of the total Hispanic population without having to share their leadership positions.*

The importance of each of these factors in making it difficult to obtain demographic information differs for each national group within the total Spanish-speaking populations. For the Cuban population, for example, illegality does not seem to be so important a factor, as this group occupies a somewhat unique political status—Cubans are able to declare themselves political refugees and avoid deportation.

In spite of the difficulties of making any such estimates, those who concern themselves with ascertaining population statistics of the Spanish-speaking population generally estimate the total to be slightly less than two million in the New York metropolitan area. Of this it is thought that only about half, or 985,000, are of Puerto Rican origin. (See Velillia 1967; Benton and Bowles 1966; Charles Unaue Associates 1969; New York State Division of Human Rights 1969.)

---

* An example of this may be cited in ASPIRA, an organization devoted to developing interests and avenues for Spanish-speaking high school students to attend post-high school educational institutions. The aim of its almost exclusively Puerto Rican leadership is to promote the advancement of Puerto Ricans. Because of funding regulations at the Federal level, it cannot be exclusive in its membership and remain oriented toward a specific national or ethnic group. Consequently, its clientele is estimated to be about 35 to 40 percent non-Puerto Rican, including a few non-Hispanos. However, in all public statements ASPIRA leaders speak exclusively of their Puerto Rican mission and will admit to the "other" segment only when confronted directly with an inquiry that does not allow for obfuscation.

THE DOMINICAN POPULATION

Published estimates of the Dominican population vary enormously, ranging from 50,000 to 185,000. The lower figure is the number reported as registered with the INS under the Alien Registration Act (INS 1972). The higher number is frequently reported in newspaper accounts, especially those quoting politically oriented figures who wish to impress *La comunidad dominicana en Nueva York* with its own size and importance; the figure probably stems from an estimate of the total Dominican population in the U.S. made by the American Consul General in Santo Domingo.

Unfortunately, alien address reports are not accurate reflections of the population present. Since within the bureaucracy of INS there seems to be no automatic process of cross-checking registrants against immigration records, it is possible for individuals simply to ignore the whole requirement with impunity. Obviously, for example, an individual living here on an expired visitor's visa will avoid the exposure implicit in completing the information on the registration form. While informants described the actions of INS agents in a variety of situations, no one ever mentioned prosecution for failure to register; they do not perceive this form of violation of the law as a possible threat. Rather, the self-identification implied in the response process is seen as having greater potential for problems, especially for the individuals in the United States illegally.

Even though the figure of 50,000 is assumed to be inaccurate because it does not coincide with the number of visas issued (Table I) or the number of arrivals and departures of Dominican nationals, the examination of annual registration reports over the past decade does indicate the growth trend of the population of Dominican citizens residing in the U.S. (Table II).

The Census of 1970 indicated that 66,914 persons, either native to the Dominican Republic or whose parents were from there, resided in New York City; of these, 51,231 were born in the Republic (Bureau of Census 1972). Using this same ratio of foreign-born to first-generation (i.e., one or both parents born in the Dominican Republic) respondents, it is possible to extrapolate that with 110,000 persons receiving visas in the decade 1963–1972, of whom 70 percent live in New York, at least 100,000 ethnic Dominicans are legally living in New York. This is assumed to be a conservative approximation and to this number must be added those living here without benefit of accepted immigrant status.

Probably the best current population estimates concerning Dominicans have been made by the marketing media. Information of this

TABLE I. IMMIGRANT VISAS ISSUED TO CITIZENS OF DOMINICAN REPUBLIC

Year	Number	Major Event
1957	1,042	
1958	1,126	
1959	803	
1960	756	
1961	3,045	Trujillo's death
1962	4,603	
1963	10,683	
1964	7,537	U.S. intervention
1965	9,504	
1966	16,503	
1967	11,514	
1968	9,250	
1969	10,670	
1970	10,807	
1971	12,626	
1972	10,760	
Total	117,853	

Source: INS Annual Reports

type is invaluable to advertisers and thus, at least some of the agencies are alert to the collection of such data. Undoubtedly, the most complete survey of the Spanish market is that done by Velillia (1967). Purportedly based upon sampling techniques not relying on census projections, he estimated that in 1966 there were 125,000 Dominicans

TABLE II. ANNUAL ALIEN ADDRESS REPORTS CITIZENS OF DOMINICAN REPUBLIC

Year	Total U.S.	New York	New Jersey
1962	12,927	9,965	264
1963	18,834	13,812	408
1964	23,269	17,830	508
1965	28,342	21,572	682
1966	38,227	27,402	1,016
1967	52,007	35,924	1,362
1968	56,585	39,579	1,632
1969	55,501	39,983	2,142
1970	71,899	49,489	2,313
1971	57,514	33,146	2,593
1972	75,501	50,465	3,152

Source: INS Annual Reports

residing in the five boroughs of New York and in adjacent New Jersey counties. This represents twelve percent of the entire non-Puerto Rican Spanish-speaking population (Table III).

TABLE III. NON-PUERTO RICAN SPANISH SPEAKERS IN
NY AREA COUNTRY OF ORIGIN

Country	Est. Numbers	% of Total
Cuba	379,000	37.9
Spain °	149,000	14.4
Dominican Republic	125,000	12.1
Argentina	63,000	6.1
Colombia	59,000	5.7
Panama	57,000	5.5
Mexico	49,000	4.7
Ecuador	31,000	3.0
Venezuela	25,000	2.4
Honduras	19,000	1.8
Peru	17,000	1.6
Chile	15,000	1.5

° A general category including all those not from listed countries.

Source: Velillia 1967

While many persons remain skeptical of such figures, there are a number of reasons to believe they more nearly approximate the actual numbers than does any other single index. The American Consul General in Santo Domingo has publicly stated that his office estimates approximately 185,000 Dominicans live in American territory (*El Caribe*, February 11, 1969). Assuming registration and nonregistration were equally distributed throughout the U.S., and applying it to this Consular figure, then the estimate by Velillia is not out of line. However, this estimate was based upon sampling done in late 1966 and the wave of immigration was only cresting at this time (see Table I).

It is generally conceded that prior to 1960 the Dominican population in the U.S. was quite small. The U.S. Census of that year lists fewer than 14,000. During the 30-year Trujillo regime, from 1930 to 1960, it was extremely difficult for a Dominican citizen to obtain a passport. In the subsequent ten years only 3,356 Dominican citizens were naturalized as citizens of the United States. Thus, the numbers naturalized do not account for the gaping discrepancy between the number of persons legally admitted to the United States, the number of alien persons reported to be here, and the much larger number apparently living in New York. Part of the discrepancy can be explained through those illegally present.

NONIMMIGRANT ENTRANTS INTO THE U.S.

The statistics on admittance to the U.S. of temporary visitors from the Dominican Republic account for the large numbers who enter and continue to reside in New York. It was the estimate of the American Consul in Santo Domingo that in 1969 at least 35,000 Dominicans who had originally arrived in the United States as visitors were currently residing in the U.S. illegally, having violated the terms of their tourist visas (*El Caribe*, February 11, 1969). Table IV indicates the large

TABLE IV. TEMPORARY VISITORS ADMITTED FROM THE
DOMINICAN REPUBLIC

Year	Number	New York	San Juan	Miami
1959	3,409			
1960	2,820			
1961	6,940			
1962	13,487			
1963	45,584			
1964	49,154			
1965	36,018			
1966	47,482			
1967	51,543			
1968	46,992	6,846	37,820	3,605
1969	56,577	9,280	42,756	4,887
1970	57,704	12,418	39,839	4,331
1971	49,652	9,002	37,010	4,031
1972	50,217	6,867	36,512	5,851

Source: INS Annual Reports

number of individuals arriving in United States territory as visitors from a nation which has only four million inhabitants. In relation to all other nations of the world, the Dominican Republic ranks tenth both in the number of temporary visitors admitted in the year 1972 and in the total number of temporary visas issued over the past decade.

All these visitors do not come to the U.S. mainland; there is considerable economic and social interchange between the two islands of Puerto Rico and Hispaniola. Perhaps indicative of the extent of this interisland travel is the regular advertisement of San Juan hotels in Santiago movie houses.

The most direct and convenient route from Santo Domingo to New York is the flights connecting the two cities; traveling via San Juan is slightly cheaper but far more time consuming. It is one of the chief surreptitious routes to the mainland. Consequently, for at least some who enter Puerto Rico, San Juan is but a temporary step on the way to New York.

CIRCULAR TRAFFIC

There is one further statistic which should be noted as indicative of the large number of Dominicans in the U.S. as well as of the numerous return visits by immigrants. In 1972, in addition to the entrance of over 10,000 persons with newly acquired residence visas and 50,000 temporary visitors from the Dominican Republic, 58,013 persons entered in the category of returning resident aliens. In other words, 58,000 Dominican citizens who are supposedly full-time residents of the United States visited the Dominican Republic and returned in one year. However, the direction and nature of this traffic is reversed for a significant number of these travelers. Regulations concerning the retention of a residence visa require that a holder of such a visa must reside primarily in the U.S., but this only means an individual must have been in the U.S. at some time during a calendar year. Consequently, an additional 1,414 who actually reside in the Dominican Republic made their annual visit to the U.S. to fulfill the requirements.

Thus, in order to account for the number of Dominican aliens residing in New York above the number who have been granted residence visas, it must be assumed that perhaps as many as one-third, if not more, are doing so *afuera de la ley* (outside the law), or as they more often put it, are here *sucio* (literally, dirty as opposed to *limpio*, or clean, without the stain of illegality). The statistical tables can tell little more about the nature of those who are here illegally. At this point, suffice it to say that they tend to be young unattached adults, since their position necessitates a degree of mobility as well as placing restraints on their ability to accept responsible roles in a household. Of such frequency is the pattern of return to the Dominican Republic that anyone who deviates from it might be suspected of being here illegally and unable to leave for fear of not being able to return.

OCCUPATIONS AT THE TIME OF ENTRY

The official statistical materials published by INS tell little of the occupational experience of the Dominican immigrant. Most who arrive seeking employment do so as unskilled workers; lack of knowledge of English and minimal literacy in Spanish preclude many from seeking employment in the areas in which they have skills and experience. Existing published material concerns aliens with professional and related occupations and indicates that relatively fewer Dominicans arrive with such skills than do other immigrant groups. In 1972, thirteen percent of the entire immigrant population coming into the U.S. fell into this category, yet only 3.5 percent of Dominicans did so (Table V).

TABLE V. MAJOR OCCUPATIONS OF DOMINICAN IMMIGRANTS 1972

	Number	Percent
Professional, technical, and kindred workers	349	3.2
Farmers and farm managers	4	—
Managers, officials, and kindred	319	3.0
Clerical	239	2.2
Sales	33	—
Craftsmen, foremen	623	5.8
Operatives	1,260	11.7
Private household workers	519	4.8
Service except private household	426	4.0
Farm laborers and foremen	297	2.8
Laborers except farm and mine	274	2.5
Housewives, children and others with no occupation	6,417	59.6

Source: INS 1972

Age Distribution of Legal Migrants

A comparative examination of population age distributions between the Dominican national population, the New York City general population, and the Dominican visa recipients reveals important contrasts. The New York City population profile is atypical because the distribution for each ten-year age cohort is remarkably similar. In the Dominican Republic the pyramidal shape of the distribution, with 34 percent of the total population less than ten years of age, is also atypical. In contrast, 63 percent of the Dominican immigrant population is in the cohorts aged 10 through 39. However, 48 percent of the immigrants are less than 20 years old, and 30 percent are from ten to nineteen years old. These figures are especially relevant to the problems considered in this book, for they indicate how many are in the age group in which formal education normally takes place.

CONCLUSION

In summary, something of the demographic dimensions of the Dominican population in New York has been shown through the use of available statistical material.

There were in 1970 more than 140,000 Dominicans in New York City.

It is apparent that since it is possible to account for less than 100,000 residing here legally, a large but unknown number remains in some illegal status. Many individuals have valid visitors' visas, but violate their status by working, thus placing them in jeopardy of deportation.

The overwhelming majority of this group has come to New York very recently—within the last decade.

The population is young, with 48 percent less than 20 years old. Only 30 percent of the general New York population is in this age category.

Dominicans come with fewer occupational skills than do other immigrants. It can be assumed that they consequently are mostly relegated to untrained and unskilled jobs.

Disregarding the individuals who may come as temporary visitors and remain, the number of visitors in the U.S. from the Dominican Republic is remarkable. The constant contact between the countries has significant sociological implications as it serves to preserve and reinforce existing social linkages between the sending and receiving societies.

These conclusions are based on information available about only a segment of this immigrant group. Available demographic statistics tell us little, if anything, about the illegal residents and workers here.

Appendix B

ANNUAL CENSUS OF NEW YORK CITY SCHOOL POPULATION IN TERMS OF THE CLASSIFICATION USED BEFORE 1968

Level and Year	Number of Pupils				Percent of Total Register		
	Puerto Rican	Negro	Others	Total	Puerto Rican	Negro	Others
Elementary							
1961	106,768	150,195	316,159	573,122	18.6	26.2	55.2
1962	111,295	158,770	311,690	581,755	19.1	27.3	53.6
1963	116,227	168,136	301,683	586,046	19.8	28.7	51.5
1964	120,168	178,208	292,772	591,148	20.3	30.2	49.5
1965	129,857	183,268	278,919	592,044	21.9	30.9	47.2
1966	138,535	192,120	268,873	599,528	23.1	32.0	44.9
1967	147,000	199,180	261,983	608,163	24.2	32.8	43.0
1968	145,724	209,933	254,942	610,599	23.8	34.4	41.8
1969	150,058	215,902	245,542	611,502	24.5	35.3	40.2
1970	154,917	219,459	240,788	615,164	25.2	35.7	39.1
Junior High							
1961	33,974	44,009	108,130	186,113	18.3	23.6	58.1
1962	35,071	49,667	108,555	193,293	18.1	25.7	56.2
1963	37,189	56,057	114,931	208,177	17.9	26.9	55.2
1964	39,474	59,330	113,273	212,077	18.6	28.0	53.4
1965	43,833	58,861	109,470	212,164	20.7	27.7	51.6
1966	45,899	61,680	105,369	212,948	21.5	29.0	49.5
1967	52,437	66,239	103,532	222,208	23.6	29.8	46.6
1968	49,732	75,896	102,818	228,446	21.8	33.2	45.0
1969	51,054	79,790	98,067	228,911	22.3	34.9	42.8
1970	52,977	83,958	95,550	232,485	22.8	36.1	41.1
Academic High							
1961	10,914	22,270	105,072	198,256	5.5	11.2	83.3
1962	12,241	22,728	167,502	205,971	6.2	12.5	81.3
1963	14,727	30,080	159,268	204,075	7.2	14.7	78.1
1964	17,851	37,167	149,134	204,152	8.7	18.2	73.1
1965	24,191	45,189	143,309	212,689	11.4	21.2	67.4
1966	28,167	48,776	147,096	224,039	12.6	21.8	65.6
1967	29,908	53,171	147,344	230,423	13.0	23.1	63.9
1968	31,285	59,506	145,085	235,876	13.3	25.2	61.5
1969	33,673	64,798	137,616	236,087	14.3	27.4	58.3
1970	37,167	72,563	136,387	246,117	15.1	29.5	55.4
All Schools							
1961	162,235	228,592	613,438	1,004,265	16.1	22.8	61.1
1962	169,493	246,336	611,599	1,027,428	16.5	24.0	59.5
1963	179,223	267,344	598,987	1,045,554	17.1	25.6	57.3
1964	188,886	288,560	576,755	1,054,201	17.9	27.4	54.7
1965	211,706	302,287	551,927	1,065,920	19.8	28.4	51.8
1966	226,614	317,613	540,591	1,084,818	20.9	29.3	49.8
1967	244,458	333,769	531,437	1,109,664	22.1	30.1	47.8
1968	240,746	361,480	519,696	1,121,922	21.5	32.2	46.3
1969	249,055	376,948	497,162	1,123,165	22.2	33.6	44.2
1970	260,040	392,714	488,321	1,141,075	22.8	34.4	42.8

Data for 1968 as of December 17. Data for other years as of October 31.

Appendix C

DISTRIBUTION BY GRADE AND CATEGORY OF PRIMARY PUPILS IN DOMINICAN REPUBLIC IN 1967–68

Type of School and Pupil Categories	1st	2nd	3rd	4th	5th	6th	Total
Public Urban							
New enrollees	34,053	27,273	24,097	20,969	16,868	14,283	
Repeaters	18,300 (35%)	4,105 (13%)	3,585 (13%)	2,742 (12%)	2,220 (12%)	1,852 (11%)	
Total	52,353	31,378	27,682	23,711	19,088	16,135	170,347
Semi-public Urban							
New enrollees	5,363	4,880	4,574	4,223	3,831	3,558	
Repeaters	713 (12%)	297 (6%)	224 (5%)	198 (4%)	147 (4%)	127 (4%)	
Total	6,076	5,177	4,798	4,421	3,978	3,685	28,145
Private Urban							
New enrollees	5,894	4,312	3,996	3,438	2,932	2,705	
Repeaters	609 (9%)	242 (5%)	244 (6%)	172 (5%)	121 (4%)	120 (4%)	
Total	6,503	4,554	4,240	3,610	3,053	2,825	24,785
Regular Rural							
New enrollees	94,400	59,773	38,170	20,646	11,345	6,768	
Repeaters	67,162 (42%)	18,555 (24%)	9,630 (20%)	3,886 (16%)	1,509 (12%)	632 (9%)	
Total	161,562	78,800	24,532	12,532	12,854	7,400	332,476
Coffee Area Rural							
New enrollees	21,017	13,249	8,712	4,084	2,137	1,031	
Repeaters	14,848 (41%)	4,290 (24%)	2,121 (20%)	690 (14%)	249 (10%)	80 (7%)	
Total	35,865	17,539	10,833	4,774	2,386	1,111	72,508

Source: Secretary of Education, Compendio Estadistico 1968

Appendix D

Annual Census of School Population Distribution by Borough, October 30, 1970

Borough	Number of Pupils							Percent of Total Register					
	Puerto Rican	Other Span. Sur. Amer.	Negro	Amer. Indian	Oriental	Others	Total	Puerto Rican	Other Span. Sur. Amer.	Negro	Amer. Indian	Oriental	Others
Elementary Schools													
Manhattan	31,873	7,968	36,097	15	4,419	12,171	92,543	34.4	8.6	39.0	0.0*	4.8	13.2
Bronx	59,957	3,450	48,677	23	922	26,987	140,016	42.8	2.5	34.8	0.0*	0.6	19.3
Brooklyn	57,894	4,291	94,184	69	1,725	69,406	227,569	25.4	1.9	41.4	0.0*	0.8	30.5
Queens	4,388	7,503	37,874	24	2,717	75,566	128,072	3.4	5.9	29.6	0.0*	2.1	59.0
Richmond	805	289	2,627	6	162	23,075	26,964	3.0	1.1	9.7	0.0*	0.6	85.6
Sub-total	154,917	23,501	219,459	137	9,945	207,205	615,164	25.2	3.8	35.7	0.0*	1.6	33.7
Special Schools	2,227	151	3,880	1	22	1,842	8,123	27.4	1.8	47.8	0.0*	0.3	22.7
City-wide	157,144	23,652	223,339	138	9,967	209,047	623,287	25.2	3.8	35.8	0.0*	1.6	33.6
Junior High Intermediate Schools													
Manhattan	11,671	2,302	14,743	4	1,755	3,706	34,181	34.2	6.7	43.1	0.0*	5.1	10.9
Bronx	19,060	1,174	16,973	11	307	11,545	49,070	38.9	2.4	34.6	0.0*	0.6	23.5
Brooklyn	20,151	1,312	36,330	29	634	29,926	88,382	22.8	1.5	41.1	0.0*	0.7	33.9
Queens	1,831	2,340	15,142	14	800	30,725	50,852	3.6	4.6	29.8	0.1*	1.6	60.4
Richmond	264	87	770	7	32	8,840	10,000	2.6	0.9	7.7	0.1*	0.3	88.4
Sub-total	52,977	7,215	83,958	65	3,528	84,742	232,485	22.8	3.1	36.1	0.0*	1.5	36.5
Special Schools	35	7	10	0	0	23	75	46.7	9.3	13.3	0.0*	0.0*	30.7
City-wide	53,012	7,222	83,968	65	3,528	84,765	232,560	22.8	3.1	36.1	0.0*	1.5	36.5
Academic High Schools													
Manhattan	10,963	2,562	14,573	15	1,460	7,307	36,880	29.7	7.0	39.5	0.0*	4.0	19.8
Bronx	12,215	976	13,350	30	374	15,762	42,707	28.6	2.3	31.3	0.1	0.8	36.9
Brooklyn	11,462	1,427	28,335	52	913	46,214	88,403	13.0	1.6	32.1	0.1	1.0	52.2
Queens	2,222	2,516	15,421	22	754	44,714	65,649	3.4	3.8	23.5	0.0*	1.2	68.1
Richmond	305	124	884	1	49	11,115	12,478	2.4	1.0	7.1	0.0*	0.4	89.1
City-wide	37,167	7,605	72,563	120	3,550	125,112	246,117	15.1	3.1	29.5	0.0*	1.5	50.8
Voc. High Schools													
Manhattan	3,704	315	4,028	7	194	3,262	11,510	32.2	2.7	35.0	0.1	1.7	28.3
Bronx	3,301	82	2,202	2	12	599	6,198	53.3	1.3	35.5	0.0*	0.2	9.7
Brooklyn	4,665	204	5,118	15	158	3,821	13,981	33.4	1.5	36.6	0.1*	1.1	27.3
Queens	994	150	1,367	1	80	3,883	6,476	15.4	2.3	21.6	0.0*	1.2	60.0
Richmond	53	10	129	0	2	752	946	5.6	1.1	13.6	0.0*	0.2	79.5
City-wide	12,717	761	12,844	26	446	12,317	39,111	32.5	2.0	32.8	0.1	1.1	31.5

* Less than 1/10 of one percent.

Bibliography

Books and Articles

Abu-Lughod, Janet
    1967   "Migrant Adjustment to City Life: The Egyptian Case." *Peasant Society: A Reader*, Jack Potter, Mary Diaz, and George Foster (eds.). Boston: Little, Brown.

Alvarez, José Hernandez
    1967   *Return Migration to Puerto Rico.* Berkeley: Institute of International Studies, University of California.

Anderson, Robert T.
    1971   "Voluntary Associations in History." *American Anthropologist,* 73(1): 209–222.

Antonini, Gustavo
    1968   "Process and Patterns of Landscape Change in the Linea Noroeste Dominican Republic." Unpublished Ph.D. dissertation, Columbia University.

Barnes, J. A.
    1954   "Classes and Committees in a Norwegian Island Parish." *Human Relations,* 7(1): 39–58.

Barth, Frederick, ed.
    1970   *Ethnic Groups and Boundaries.* London: Allen and Unwin.

Benton and Bowles, Inc.
    1966   "The Spanish Language Market." *Media Report,* no. 13, December 15, 1966.

Charles Unaue Associates
    1969   "The Spanish Speaking Market in the United States." September. Mimeo.

Cohen, Abner
    1969   *Customs and Politics in Urban Africa.* Berkeley: University of California Press.

Cordasco, Francesco and Eugene Bucchioni (eds.)
    1968   *Puerto Rican Children in Mainland Schools. A Sourcebook for Teachers.* Metuchen, N.J.: Scarecrow Press.

Cordasco, Frank M. and Leonard Covello (comps.)
    1967   "Studies of Puerto Rican Children in American Schools—A Preliminary Bibliography." *Congressional Record,* October 31, *13*(176).

Cremin, Lawrence
    1961   *The Transformation of the School.* New York: Knopf.

Doughty, Paul L.
    1970   "Behind the Back of the City: 'Provincial' Life in Lima, Peru." *Peasants in Cities,* William Mangin (ed.). Boston: Houghton Mifflin.

Fitzpatrick, Joseph P.
    1968   "Puerto Ricans in Perspective: The Meaning of Migration to the Mainland." *International Migration Review,* 2: 7–20.

Franco, Franklyn J.
    1969   *Los Negros, Los Mulatos y la Nacion Dominicana.* Santo Domingo: Editora Nacional.

Glazier, Nathan and Daniel P. Moynihan
    1963   *Beyond the Melting Pot.* Cambridge, Mass.: M.I.T. Press.

Gluckman, Max
    1958   *Analysis of a Social Situation in Modern Zululand.* Rhodes-Livingston. Paper no. 10.

Gonzales, Nancie Solien
    1971   "Peasants Progress: Dominicans in New York." *Caribbean Studies,* *10*(3): 154–171.

Greer, Colin
    1969   "Immigrants, Negroes and the Public Schools." *Urban Review,* *3*(4): 9–12.

Handlin, Oscar
    1959   *The Newcomers: Negroes and Puerto Ricans in American Life.* Boston: Harvard University Press.

Hendricks, Glenn
    1968   "The British West Indian Immigrant Group in Puerto Plata." Teachers College, Columbia University Team. University Consortium for Caribbean Research and Training. Offset.
    1973   "La Raza en Nueva York: Social Pluralism and Schools." *Teachers College Record,* 74(3): 379–393.

Herskovits, Melville J. and Frances S.
    1947   *Trinidad Village.* New York: Knopf.

Kapferer, B.
1969   "Norms and the Manipulation of Relationships in a Work Context." *Social Networks in Urban Situations,* J. Clyde Mitchell (ed.). London: Manchester University Press.

Katzin, M. F.
1959   "The Jamaican Country Higgler." *Social and Economic Studies, 8*(4): 421–440.

Latorre, Eduardo, et al
1969   "Bonao: Una Ciudad Dominicana." Santiago: Universidad Catolica Madre Y Maestra. Mimeo.

Little, Kenneth
1965   *West African Urbanization: A Study of Voluntary Associations in Social Change.* London: Cambridge University Press.

Lowenthal, Abraham F.
1969   "The Dominican Republic: The Politics of Chaos." *Reform and Revolution: Readings in Latin American Politics,* Arpad von Lazar and Robert R. Kaufman (eds.). Boston: Allyn and Bacon.

Mangin, William (ed.)
1970   *Peasants in Cities.* New York: Houghton Mifflin.

Mayer, Adrian
1967   "Patrons and Brokers. Rural Leadership in Four Overseas Indian Communities," in *Essays Presented to Raymond Firth,* Maurice Freedman (ed.). Chicago: Aldine.

Meillassoux, Claude
1968   *Urbanization of an African Community: Voluntary Associations in Bomako.* Seattle: University of Washington Press.

Ortega, Manuel M.
1971   "Population Control Policies in the Dominican Republic." Paper delivered at the annual meeting of the Society for Applied Anthropology, Miami. Mimeo.

Polgar, Steven
1960   "Biculturalism of Mesquakie Boys." *American Anthropologist, 62:* 217–235.

Pritzher, Leon and N. D. Rothwell
1967   *Procedural Difficulties in Taking Past Censuses in Predominantly Negro, Puerto Rican, and Mexican Areas.* Washington: U.S. Dept. of Commerce, Bureau of the Census.

Redfield, R., R. Linton, and M. J. Herskovits
1936   "A Memorandum for the Study of Acculturation." *American Anthropologist, 38:* 149–152.

Roberts, T. D.
    1966   *Area Handbook of the Dominican Republic.* Washington: Government Printing Office.

Sexton, Patricia C.
    1965   *Spanish Harlem, Anatomy of Poverty.* New York: Harper and Row.

Spicer, Edward A.
    1961   *Perspectives in American Indian Culture Change.* Chicago: University of Chicago Press.

Spradley, James P.
    1972   "Adaptive Strategies of Urban Nomads: The Ethnoscience of Tramp Culture." *The Anthropology of Urban Environments,* Thomas Weaver and Douglas White (eds.). Boulder, Colo.: Society for Applied Anthropology Monograph no. 11.

Velillia, Martin
    1967   *2,000,000 to Captivate.* New York: Thunder Book.

Vincent, Joan
    1970   "The Politics of Ethnicity: An Outline of a Situation-and-Event Approach." Paper presented at the annual meeting of the Society for Applied Anthropology, Boulder, Colo. Mimeo.

Wagley, Charles
    1968   *The Latin American Tradition.* New York: Columbia Unisity Press.

Walker, Malcolm T.
    1972   *Politics and the Power Structure: A Rural Community in the Dominican Republic.* New York: Teachers College Press.

Whitten, Norman E., Jr.
    1965   *Class, Kinship, and Power in an Ecuadorian Town.* Stanford, Calif.: Stanford University Press.

Wiarda, Howard J.
    1969   *The Dominican Republic: Nation in Transition.* New York: Praeger.

Wildes, Leon
    1968   *Obtaining Permanent Residence for Aliens: Handbook on Immigration and Naturalization.* New York: Practicing Law Institute.

Wipfler, William Louis
    1964   "The Churches of the Dominican Republic in the Light of History." Unpublished dissertation, Union Theological Seminary, New York.

Wolfe, Eric
>   1956   "Aspects of Group Relations in Complex Societies: Mexico."
>   *American Anthrolopolgist, 58:* 1065–75.

Government Documents

Dirección General de Educación Adultos
>   1968   *Plan Nacional de Alfabetización y Educación de Adultos.*
>   Secretaria de Estado de Educación Bellas Artes y Cultos:
>   Santo Domingo.

New York City Board of Education
>   1970   *Annual Census of School Population, October 31, 1969.* Pub-
>   lication 330.
>   1971   *Annual Census of School Population, October 30, 1970.* Pub-
>   lication 340.

New York State Division of Human Rights
>   1969   *Puerto Ricans in New York State.*

Oficina de Programación Educativa
>   1968   "Primer Censo Nacional de Educación." *Locales Escolares de
>   Enseñanza Oficial.* Santo Domingo: Secretaría de Estado
>   de Educación Bellas Artes y Cultos.

Oficina Nacional de Estradística
>   1966   *Cuarto Censo Nacional de Población.* Resume General. Santo
>   Domingo.
>   1967   *Republica Dominicana en Cifras.* Santo Domingo.
>   1970   *Cifras Oficiales Preliminares.* Boletín no. 5, Julio 1970. Santo
>   Domingo.

Secretary of Education
>   1968   *Compendio Estadístico: 3.* Santo Domingo.

U.S. Agency for International Development
>   1967   *Dominican Republic Annual Report.*

U.S. Bureau of Census
>   1963   *U.S. Census of Population: 1960.* Vol. I, *Characteristics of
>   the Population, Part 34, New York.* Washington: Govern-
>   ment Printing Office.
>   1970   *1970 Census of Population, Preliminary Reports.* Washing-
>   ton: Government Printing Office.
>   1972   *U.S. Census of Population: 1970. Detailed Characteristics
>   Final Report, PC(1)-D34 New York.* Washington: Gov-
>   ernment Printing Office.

U.S. Department of Labor
>   1968   *Labor Law and Practice in the Dominican Republic* Bureau
>   of Labor Statistics, Report 343. Washington: Govern-
>   ment Printing Office.

U.S. Immigration and Naturalization Service
  1966   *Annual Report.* Washington: Government Printing Office.
  1968
  1969
  1970
  1971
  1972

U.S. Select Commission on Western Hemisphere Immigration
  1968   *Report.* Washington: Government Printing Office.

Newspapers and Periodicals

Cachafu, Santo Domingo
  1969   Cartoon of Vice Consul, June 9.

El Caribe, Santo Domingo
  1969   "Indica 35,000 Dominicanos Viven Ilegalmente en los Estados
          Unidos," February 11.
  1969   "Hace lo Posible de Evitar Fraudes," February 14.
  1969   "Pide Descontinuar Sistema Educativo," February 20.
  1969   "Deportan 5 Dominican Tras 4 Meses de Arresto," October
          21.
  1969   "34 Dominicanos Encaran Odisea," October 27.

El Diario, New York
  1969   "Consul Dominicano Duda Sucesora Siga Linea," August 29.

El Tiempo, New York
  1970   "Profesores Hablan un Español Macarrónico," November
          17: 6.

Listin-Diario, Santo Domingo
  1969   "Detienen Suspuestos Alteradores De Visas," February 12.

New York Times
  1970   "Dominicans Crowd 3 Roads Leading out of Poverty," May
          15.
  1970   "Prudent Dominican Leader," May 19.
  1970   "Spanglish is Spoken Here, and New School Teaches It,"
          December 28.

Index

Abu-Lughod, Janet, 106
Acción Social, 29, 35n., 121
acculturation, 1, 4, 5, 126; defined, 4n.; goal criteria of, 128
Aldea, 5, 6, 7, 21–39, 68, 94; and communication with New York, 40–43; and household relationships to New York kinsmen, 43 (table); immigrants from, *see* Aldeanos in New York; *Padres y Amigos de la Escuela* in, 37; remittances to, 42–44; returnees to, 44–49; school in, 35–39; school registration in (1969), 36 (table); social relations in, 31–35; and socialization practices for family interdependence, 102, 103
Aldeanos in New York, 24–28, 73, 75, 79, 80 and n., 81, 82, 91, 92, 93, 106, 112, 115, 127; and Catholic Church, 117, 118, 119, 120; and education, *see* New York schools; marital unions of, 97 (table); occupations of, 76 (table); *see also* Dominicans in New York
Alien Address Reports, 149, 152 (table)
Alien Registration Act, 151
almacén, 22, 23; defined, 22n.
Alou brothers, 114
Alvarez, José Hernandez, 79n.
Amigos de los Dominicanos, 107–08
Anderson, Robert T., 106
Antonini, Gustavo, 22n.

anthropology, urban, 2n.
ASPIRA, 107, 150n.
assimilation, 1, 4; defined, 4n.
Association of Immigration and Nationality Lawyers (AINL), 55n.
associations, voluntary, 106–16
Autonomous University of Santo Domingo (UASD), 17, 20

Balaguer, Joaquín, 15, 27, 28, 35, 84, 108, 112
Bao River, 21
Barnes, J. A., 7n.
Barth, Frederick, 141
baseball, as national sport of Dominican Republic, 114–15
Benton and Bowles, Inc., 150
biculturalism, 128
billeteros, 59
birth control, 98 and n.
bodegas, 22, 23; defined, 22n.
Bonao, 12, 95
Bosch, Juan, 15
brokers, culture, *see* culture brokers; visa, 55 and n.
Bronx, Dominican colony in, 80 and n., 82
Brooklyn, Dominican colony in, 80
buscones, 58

Cachafú, 64
campesinos, 2n., 22, 28, 49, 61, 95, 106, 115, 116, 119, 137, 142
Caribe, El, 20, 37, 62, 68, 69, 153, 154
Catholic Church, 11, 23, 28–30, 94, 98n., 110, 112n., 117–21